Ordinary People

Conversation Pieces

A Small Paperback Series from Aqueduct Press
Subscriptions available: www.aqueductpress.com

About the Aqueduct Press Conversation Pieces Series

The feminist engaged with sf is passionately interested in challenging the way things are, passionately determined to understand how everything works. It is my constant sense of our feminist-sf present as a grand conversation that enables me to trace its existence into the past and from there see its trajectory extending into our future. A genealogy for feminist sf would not constitute a chart depicting direct lineages but would offer us an ever-shifting, fluid mosaic, the individual tiles of which we will probably only ever partially access. What could be more in the spirit of feminist sf than to conceptualize a genealogy that explicitly manifests our own communities across not only space but also time?

Aqueduct's small paperback series, Conversation Pieces, aims to both document and facilitate the "grand conversation." The Conversation Pieces series presents a wide variety of texts, including short fiction (which may not always be sf and may not necessarily even be feminist), essays, speeches, manifestoes, poetry, interviews, correspondence, and group discussions. Many of the texts are reprinted material, but some are new. The grand conversation reaches at least as far back as Mary Shelley and extends, in our speculations and visions, into the continually-created future. In Jonathan Goldberg's words, "To look forward to the history that will be, one must look at and retell the history that has been told." And that is what Conversation Pieces is all about.

L. Timmel Duchamp

Jonathan Goldberg, "The History That Will Be" in Louise Fradenburg and Carla Freccero, eds., *Premodern Sexualities* (New York and London: Routledge, 1996)

Conversation Pieces
Volume 7

Ordinary People

A Collection

by

Eleanor Arnason

Published by Aqueduct Press
PO Box 95787
Seattle, WA 98145-2787
www.aqueductpress.com

ISBN: 978-0-9746559-0-1

Book Design by Kathryn Wilham
Original Block Print of Mary Shelley by Justin Kempton:
www.writersmugs.com

"The Land of Ordinary People," *Looking for Utopia*, New York,
    Schocken Books, 1985.

"The Grammarian's Five Daughters," *Realms of Fantasy*, June 1999.

"A Ceremony of Discontent," *A Room of One's Own*, Volume 6,
    Numbers 1 and 2, 1981.

"The Warlord of Saturn's Moons," *New Worlds* 6, New York.
    Avon Books, 1974.

"The Lovers," *Asimov's Science Fiction*, July 1994.

"Origin Story," *Tales of the Unanticipated*, April 2000-April 2001.

"The Small Black Box of Morality," *Tales of the Unanticipated*,
    Spring/Summer/Fall 1996.

To Jon and Sia
with Love

Contents

The Land of Ordinary People

For John Lennon

I.

Welcome to the land of ordinary people.
Our buildings are low.
Our roads are made
for bicycles not limousines.
As for our public monuments, they celebrate
achievements of day-to-day life.

Here, in the main square,
the cube of bronze
ten meters tall is for
the Unknown Inventor of Bean Curd.

And here, above the boulevard,
this line of wash
made of heavy plastic
and hung on steel—
this celebrates

the housewives and laundry maids
throughout all history.

Oh women with muscular arms
beating sheets on rocks by the river,
we honor you!
We shall not forget
your labor in the cause of cleanliness!

II.

Our streets are named for flowers and for trades.
At the moment, we stand
at the corner of Magnolia Lane
and Keypunch Avenue.
Further down
is the fountain at the start
of Plumbers' Promenade.

Notice the shape: a giant bidet
shooting jets of water
that glisten in the sunlight.

III.

Politicians?
We have none, holding—as we do—
the very name accursed.

No soldiers
nor theologians,
not even one philosopher.

But a multitude of gardeners
and potters,
mechanics
and extruders of plastic.

IV.

In the center of every town, we build
a hall—
large and lined with mirrors.
We bring our children there
on days off when it's rainy.

"Look around," we say.
"This is the source of power.
Here are the heroes.
Here are the leaders.
The ones who sing,
the ones who are sung about—
all are here.

"Look and see
how they return your gaze."

The Grammarian's
Five Daughters

Once there was a grammarian who lived in a great city that no longer exists, so we don't have to name it. Although she was learned and industrious and had a house full of books, she did not prosper. To make the situation worse, she had five daughters. Her husband, a diligent scholar with no head for business, died soon after the fifth daughter was born, and the grammarian had to raise them alone. It was a struggle, but she managed to give each an adequate education, though a dowry—essential in the grammarian's culture—was impossible. There was no way for her daughters to marry. They would become old maids, eking (their mother thought) a miserable living as scribes in the city market. The grammarian fretted and worried, until the oldest daughter was 15 years old.

Then the girl came to her mother and said, "You can't possibly support me, along with my sisters. Give me what you can, and I'll go out and seek my fortune. No matter what happens, you'll have one less mouth to feed."

The mother thought for a while, then produced a bag. "In here are nouns, which I consider the solid core and treasure of language. I give them to you because you're the oldest. Take them and do what you can with them."

The oldest daughter thanked her mother and kissed her sisters and trudged away, the bag of nouns on her back.

Time passed. She traveled as best she could, until she came to a country full of mist. Everything was shadowy and uncertain. The oldest daughter blundered along, never knowing exactly where she was, till she came to a place full of shadows that reminded her of houses.

A thin, distant voice cried out, "Oyez. The king of this land will give his son or daughter to whoever can dispel the mist."

The oldest daughter thought a while, then opened her bag. Out came the nouns, sharp and definite. *Sky* leaped up and filled the grayness overhead. *Sun* leaped up and lit the sky. *Grass* spread over the dim gray ground. *Oak* and *elm* and *poplar* rose from grass. *House* followed, along with *town* and *castle* and *king*.

Now, in the sunlight, the daughter was able to see people. Singing her praise, they escorted her to the castle, where the grateful king gave his eldest son to her. Of course they married and lived happily, producing many sharp and definite children.

In time they ruled the country, which acquired a new name: Thingnesse. It became famous for bright skies, vivid landscapes, and solid, clear-thinking citizens who loved best what they could touch and hold.

※

Now the story turns to the second daughter. Like her sister, she went to the grammarian and said, "There is no way you can support the four of us. Give me what you can, and I will go off to seek my fortune. No matter what happens, you will have one less mouth to feed."

The mother thought for a while, then produced a bag. "This contains verbs, which I consider the strength of language. I give them to you because you are my second child and the most fearless and bold. Take them and do what you can with them."

The daughter thanked her mother and kissed her sisters and trudged away, the bag of verbs on her back.

Like her older sister, the second daughter made her way as best she could, coming at last to a country of baking heat. The sun blazed in the middle of a dull blue, dusty sky. Everything she saw seemed overcome with lassitude. Honey bees, usually the busiest of creatures, rested on their hives, too stupefied to fly in search of pollen. Plowmen dozed at their plows. The oxen in front of the plows dozed as well. In the little trading towns, the traders sat in their shops, far too weary to cry their wares.

The second daughter trudged on. The bag on her back grew ever heavier and the sun beat on her head, until she could barely move or think. Finally, in a town square, she came upon a man in the embroidered tunic of a royal herald. He sat on the rim of the village fountain, one hand trailing in water.

When she came up, he stirred a bit, but was too tired to lift his head. "Oy-" he said at last, his voice whispery and slow. "The queen of this country will give—give a child in marriage to whoever can dispel this stupor."

The second daughter thought a while, then opened her bag. *Walk* jumped out, then *scamper* and *canter*, *run* and *jump* and *fly*. Like bees, the verbs buzzed through the country. The true bees roused themselves in response. So did the country's birds, farmers, oxen, housewives, and merchants. In every town, dogs began to bark. Only the cats stayed curled up, having their own schedule for sleeping and waking.

Blow blew from the bag, then *gust*. The country's banners flapped. Like a cold wind from the north or an electric storm, the verbs hummed and crackled. The daughter, amazed, held the bag open until the last slow verb had crawled out and away.

Townsfolk danced around her. The country's queen arrived on a milk-white racing camel. "Choose any of my children. You have earned a royal mate."

The royal family lined up in front of her, handsome lads and lovely maidens, all twitching and jittering, due to the influence of the verbs.

All but one, the second daughter realized: a tall maid who held herself still, though with evident effort. While the other royal children had eyes like deer or camels, this one's eyes—though dark—were keen. The grammarian's daughter turned toward her.

The maiden said, "I am the crown princess. Marry me and you will be a queen's consort. If you want children, one of my brothers will bed you. If we're lucky, we'll have a daughter to rule after I am gone. But no matter what happens, I will love you forever, for you have saved my country from inaction."

Of course, the grammarian's daughter chose this princess.

Weary of weariness and made restless by all the verbs, the people of the country became nomads, riding

7

horses and following herds of great-horned cattle over a dusty plain. The grammarian's second daughter bore her children in carts, saw them grow up on horseback, and lived happily to an energetic old age, always side by side with her spouse, the nomad queen. The country they ruled, which had no clear borders and no set capital, became known as Change.

๛

Now the story turns back to the grammarian. By this time her third daughter had reached the age of 15.

"The house has been almost roomy since my sisters left," she told her mother. "And we've had almost enough to eat. But that's no reason for me to stay, when they have gone to seek their fortunes. Give me what you can, and I will take to the highway. No matter what happens, you'll have one less mouth to feed."

"You are the loveliest and most elegant of my daughters," said the grammarian. "Therefore I will give you this bag of adjectives. Take them and do what you can with them. May luck and beauty go with you always."

The daughter thanked her mother, kissed her sisters, and trudged away, the bag of adjectives on her back. It was a difficult load to carry. At one end were words like *rosy* and *delicate*, which weighed almost nothing and fluttered. At the other end, like stones, lay *dark* and *grim* and *fearsome*. There seemed no way to balance such a collection. The daughter did the best she could, trudging womanfully along until she came to a bleak desert land. Day came suddenly here, a white sun popping into a cloudless sky. The intense light bleached colors from the earth. There was little water. The local people lived in caves and canyons to be safe from the sun.

"Our lives are bare stone," they told the grammarian's third daughter, "and the sudden alternation of blazing day and pitch-black night. We are too poor to have a king or queen, but we will give our most respected person, our shaman, as spouse to anyone who can improve our situation."

The third daughter thought for a while, then unslung her unwieldy bag, placed it on the bone-dry ground, and opened it. Out flew *rosy* and *delicate* like butterflies. *Dim* followed, looking like a moth.

"Our country will no longer be stark," cried the people with joy. "We'll have dawn and dusk, which have always been rumors."

One by one the other adjectives followed: *rich*, *subtle*, *beautiful*, *luxuriant*. This last resembled a crab covered with shaggy vegetation. As it crept over the hard ground, plants fell off it—or maybe sprang up around it—so it left a trail of greenness.

Finally, the bag was empty except for nasty words. As *slimy* reached out a tentacle, the third daughter pulled the drawstring tight. *Slimy* shrieked in pain. Below it in the bag, the worst adjectives rumbled, "Unjust! Unfair!"

The shaman, a tall, handsome person, was nearby, trying on various adjectives. He/she/it was especially interested in *masculine*, *feminine*, and *androgynous*. "I can't make up my mind," the shaman said. "This is the dark side of our new condition. Before, we had clear choices. Now, the new complexity puts all in doubt."

The sound of complaining adjectives attracted the shaman. He, she, or it came over and looked at the bag, which still had a tentacle protruding and wiggling.

"This is wrong. We asked for an end to starkness, which is not the same as asking for prettiness. In there—at the bag's bottom—are words we might need someday: *sublime*, *awesome*, *terrific*, and so on. Open it up and let them out."

"Are you certain?" asked the third daughter.

"Yes," said the shaman.

She opened the bag. Out crawled *slimy* and other words equally disgusting. The shaman nodded with approval as more and more unpleasant adjectives appeared. Last of all, after *grim* and *gruesome* and *terrific*, came *sublime*. The word shone like a diamond or a thundercloud in sunlight.

"You see," said the shaman. "Isn't that worth the rest?"

"You are a holy being," said the daughter, "and may know things I don't."

Sublime crawled off toward the mountains. The third daughter rolled up her bag. "All gone," she said. "Entirely empty."

The people looked around. Their land was still a desert, but now clouds moved across the sky, making the sunlight on bluff and mesa change. In response to this, the desert colors turned subtle and various. In the mountains rain fell, misty gray, feeding clear streams that ran in the bottoms of canyons. The vegetation there, spread by the land-crab *luxuriant* and fed by the streams, was a dozen—two dozen—shades of green.

"Our land is beautiful!" the people cried. "And you shall marry our shaman!"

But the shaman was still trying on adjectives, unable to decide if she, he, or it wanted to be feminine or masculine or androgynous.

"I can't marry someone who can't make up her mind," the third daughter said. "Subtlety is one thing. Uncertainty is another."

"In that case," the people said, "you will become our first queen, and the shaman will become your first minister."

This happened. In time the third daughter married a young hunter, and they had several children, all different in subtle ways.

The land prospered, though it was never fertile, except in the canyon bottoms. But the people were able to get by. They valued the colors of dawn and dusk, moving light on mesas, the glint of water running over stones, the flash of bugs and birds in flight, the slow drift of sheep on a hillside—like clouds under clouds. The name of their country was Subtletie. It lay north of Thingnesse and west of Change.

Back home, in the unnamed city, the grammarian's fourth daughter came of age.

"We each have a room now," she said to her mother, "and there's plenty to eat. But my sister and I still don't have dowries. I don't want to be an old maid in the marketplace. Therefore, I plan to go as my older sisters did. Give me what you can, and I'll do my best with it. And if I make my fortune, I'll send for you."

The mother thought for a while and rummaged in her study, which was almost empty. She had sold her books years before to pay for her daughters' educations;

and most of her precious words were gone. At last, she managed to fill a bag with adverbs, though they were frisky little creatures and tried to escape.

But a good grammarian can outwit any word. When the bag was close to bursting, she gave it to her fourth daughter.

"This is what I have left. I hope it will serve." The daughter thanked her mother and kissed her one remaining sister and took off along the highway, the bag of adverbs bouncing on her back.

Her journey was a long one. She made it womanfully, being the most energetic of the five daughters and the one with the most buoyant spirit. As she walked—quickly, slowly, steadily, unevenly—the bag on her back kept jouncing around and squeaking.

"What's in there?" asked other travelers. "Mice?"

"Adverbs," said the fourth daughter.

"Not much of a market for them," said the other travelers. "You'd be better off with mice."

This was plainly untrue, but the fourth daughter was not one to argue. On she went, until her shoes wore to pieces and fell from her weary feet. She sat on a stone by the highway and rubbed her bare soles, while the bag squeaked next to her.

A handsome lad in many-colored clothes stopped in front of her. "What's in the bag?" he asked.

"Adverbs," said the daughter shortly.

"Then you must, like me, be going to the new language fair."

The daughter looked up with surprise, noticing—as she did so—the lad's rosy cheeks and curling, auburn hair. "What?" she asked intently.

"I'm from the country of Subtletie and have a box of adjectives on my horse, every possible color, arranged in drawers: *aquamarine, russet, dun, crimson, puce.* I have them all. Your shoes have worn out. Climb up on my animal, and I'll give you a ride to the fair."

The fourth daughter agreed, and the handsome lad—whose name, it turned out, was Russet—led the horse to the fair. There, in booths with bright awnings, wordsmiths and merchants displayed their wares: solid nouns, vigorous verbs, subtle adjectives. But there were no adverbs.

"You have brought just the right product," said Russet enviously. "What do you say we share a booth? I'll get cages for your adverbs, who are clearly frisky little fellows, and you can help me arrange my colors in the most advantageous way."

The fourth daughter agreed; they set up a booth. In front were cages of adverbs, all squeaking and jumping, except for the sluggish ones. The lad's adjectives hung on the awning, flapping in a mild wind. As customers came by, drawn by the adverbs, Russet said, "How can we have *sky* without *blue*? How can we have *gold* without *shining*? And how much use is a verb if it can't be modified? Is *walk* enough, without *slowly* or *quickly*?

"Come and buy! Come and buy! We have *mincingly* and *angrily, knowingly, lovingly,* as well as a fine assortment of adjectives. Ride home happily with half a dozen colors and a cage full of adverbs."

The adverbs sold like hot cakes, and the adjectives sold well also. By the fair's end, both Russet and the fourth daughter were rich, and there were still plenty of adverbs left.

"They must have been breeding, though I didn't notice," said Russet. "What are you going to do with them?"

"Let them go," said the daughter.

"Why?" asked Russet sharply.

"I have enough money to provide for myself, my mother, and my younger sister. *Greedy* is an adjective and not one of my wares." She opened the cages. The adverbs ran free—*slowly*, *quickly*, *hoppingly*, *happily*. In the brushy land around the fairground, they proliferated. The region became known as Varietie. People moved there to enjoy the brisk, invigorating, varied weather, as well as the fair, which happened every year thereafter.

As for the fourth daughter, she built a fine house on a hill above the fairground. From there she could see for miles. Out back, among the bushes, she put feeding stations for the adverbs, and she sent for her mother and one remaining sister. The three of them lived together contentedly. The fourth daughter did not marry Russet, though she remained always grateful for his help. Instead, she became an old maid. It was a good life, she said, as long as one had money and respect.

In time, the fifth daughter came of age. (She was the youngest by far.) Her sister offered her a dowry, but she said, "I will do no less than the rest of you. Let my mother give me whatever she has left, and I will go to seek my fortune."

The mother went into her study, full of new books now, and looked around. "I have a new collection of nouns," she told the youngest daughter.

"No, for my oldest sister took those and did well with them, from all reports. I don't want to repeat someone else's adventures."

Verbs were too active, she told her mother, and adjectives too varied and subtle. "I'm a plain person who likes order and organization."

"How about adverbs?" asked the mother.

"Is there nothing else?"

"Prepositions," said the mother, and showed them to her daughter. They were dull little words, like something a smith might make from pieces of iron rod. Some were bent into angles. Others were curved into hooks. Still others were circles or helixes. Something about them touched the youngest daughter's heart.

"I'll take them," she said and put them in a bag. Then she thanked her mother, kissed her sister, and set off.

Although they were small, the prepositions were heavy and had sharp corners. The youngest daughter did not enjoy carrying them, but she was a methodical person who did what she set out to do. Tromp, tromp, she went along the highway, which wound finally into a broken country, full of fissures and jagged peaks. The local geology was equally chaotic. Igneous rocks intruded into sedimentary layers. New rock lay under old rock. The youngest daughter, who loved order, had never seen such a mess. While neat, she was also rational, and she realized she could not organize an entire mountain range. "Let it be what it is," she said. "My concern is my own life and other people."

The road grew rougher and less maintained. Trails split off from it and sometimes rejoined it or ended nowhere, as the daughter discovered by trial. "This country needs engineers," she muttered peevishly. (A few adverbs had hidden among the prepositions and would pop out now and then. *Peevishly* was one.)

At length the road became nothing more than a path, zigzagging down a crumbling mountain slope. Below her in a valley was a town of shacks, though town might be the wrong word. The shacks were scattered helter-skelter over the valley bottom and up the valley sides. Nothing was seemly or organized. Pursing her lips—a trick she had learned from her mother, who did it when faced by a sentence that would not parse—the fifth daughter went down the path.

When she reached the valley floor, she saw people running to and fro.

"Madness," said the daughter. The prepositions, in their bag, made a sound of agreement like metal chimes.

In front of her, two women began to argue—over what she could not tell.

"Explain," cried the fifth daughter, while the prepositions went "bong" and "bing."

"Here in the Canton of Chaos nothing is capable of agreement," one woman said. "Is it age before beauty, or beauty before age? What came first, the chicken or the egg? Does might make right, and if so, what is left?"

"This is certainly madness," said the daughter.

"How can we disagree?" said the second woman. "We live topsy-turvy and pell-mell, with no hope of anything better." Saying this, she hit the first woman on the head with a live chicken.

"Egg!" cried the first woman.

"Left!" cried the second.

The chicken squawked, and the grammarian's last daughter opened her bag.

Out came the prepositions: *of, to, from, with, at, by, in, under, over,* and so on. When she'd put them into the bag, they had seemed like hooks or angles. Now, departing in orderly rows, they reminded her of ants. Granted, they were large ants, each one the size of a woman's hand, their bodies metallic gray, their eyes like cut and polished hematite. A pair of tongs or pincers protruded from their mouths; their thin legs, moving delicately over the ground, seemed made of iron rods or wire.

Somehow—it must have been magic—the things they passed over and around became organized. Shacks turned into tidy cottages. Winding paths became streets. The fields were square now. The trees ran in lines along the streets and roads. Terraces appeared on the mountainsides.

The mountains themselves remained as crazy as ever, strata sideways and upside down. "There is always a limit to order," said the daughter. At her feet, a handful of remaining prepositions chimed their agreement like bells.

In decorous groups, the locals came up to her. "You have saved us from utter confusion. We are a republic, so we can't offer you a throne. But please become our first citizen, and if you want to marry, please accept any of us. Whatever you do, don't go away, unless you leave these ingenious little creatures that have connected us with one another."

"I will stay," said the fifth daughter, "and open a grammar school. As for marriage, let that happen as it will."

The citizens agreed by acclamation to her plan. She settled in a tidy cottage and opened a tidy school, where the canton's children learned grammar.

In time, she married four other schoolteachers. (Due to the presence of the prepositions, which remained in their valley and throughout the mountains, the local people developed a genius for creating complex social groups. Their diagrams of kinship excited the awe of neighbors, and their marriages grew more intricate with each generation.)

The land became known as Relation. In addition to genealogists and marriage brokers, it produced diplomats and merchants. These last two groups, through trade and negotiation, gradually unified the five countries of Thingnesse, Change, Subtletie, Varietie, and Relation. The empire they formed was named Cooperation. No place was more solid, more strong, more complex, more energetic, or better organized.

The flag of the new nation was an ant under a blazing yellow sun. Sometimes the creature held a tool: a pruning hook, scythe, hammer, trowel, or pen. At other times its hands (or feet) were empty. Always below it was the nation's motto:

WITH.

A Ceremony of Discontent

Vusai woke at sunrise. The sky was overcast, and the air had the smell of rain. She got up and took down her hammock. Quickly she folded it and put it away. Then came the curtains along the edge of the veranda. They had come from Hui, the village with the best weavers. They were thin and completely transparent, except where the pattern was. The pattern was a zigzag, done in white and green. At the bottom the curtains were tied to the floor, so bugs couldn't fly in under them. She undid the ties and pulled the curtains up. Then she went inside. The rest of her family was there: her husband Mawl and Shaitu, the wife who had children. Mawl was cooking breakfast, Shaitu was doing nothing. She was pregnant again, round, fat, and pleased with herself. Vusai had never understood her attitude. What was so fine about bulging out and becoming clumsy? Who would want such a thing? Vusai helped herself to a piece of bread, then looked around for the children. They were in a corner: a green heap of naked bodies, all tangled up with one another, wrestling fiercely and silently. All girls and fine ones. When the time for the choice came, she knew what it would be. They were too independent to be mothers.

She sat down. Mawl gave her a bowl. She dipped the bread in and took a bite. Ah! That burned like the sun! It took the bad taste out of her mouth, and it even lightened her mood a little. The day seemed less grey.

"I have made a decision," she said.

"Yes?" said Mawl.

Shaitu blinked and looked interested.

"I am going to ask for a ceremony." She finished the bread and took another piece.

"What kind of ceremony?"

"A ceremony of discontent."

Mawl looked surprised.

Shaitu asked, "But why? Your pottery is going well. Did you hear about the people from Hui? They asked for your work by name. They wanted pots by Vusai, they told the trading chieftainess."

"I know."

"Are you unhappy with the family?" asked Mawl. He sounded anxious. He was the kind of man who always worried about his wives and his children too.

Vusai told him, "No. I do not know exactly what is wrong. But nothing looks right to me. Everything has a nick or scratch or an imperfection of color. I hear false notes when you sing, Mawl. And you, Shaitu, the sight of you enrages me. I think, why is she happy?"

"Maybe it's the rain," Mawl said. "You have never liked this time of year."

"No." Shaitu leaned forward. "She is discontented. I know the signs. She has been restless since the harvest, and it was dry then. Remember when she broke the pot? The big one that was as blue as the sky? She said it had a flaw. It didn't. I have seen this before."

Mawl looked uneasy. Everyone knew about Shaitu's mother. She had gone crazy and abandoned her family, in order to make fishing nets. It was all due to uncertainty and discontent. No one had noticed the first signs, and by the time the ceremony was done, it was too late.

"Very well," he said. "Go to the chieftain in charge of ceremonies. I will contribute three boxes of dried fish."

"I will contribute food from the garden," Shaitu said. "And take him the pot that is spotted white and brown."

Vusai got up. "Thank you." She still felt angry. Shaitu was comparing her to the crazy woman who made nets. She was certain of it. She left the house. It was raining now, a steady drizzle. She walked down the muddy street. One of the village birds followed her. It was a big creature, almost as tall as she was. It had long legs and a long neck and a tiny head. It wanted food, and it was too stupid to realize she wasn't a mother. Only mothers fed the birds.

"Go away, you stupid thing!" she told it.

It followed her all the way to the house of the chieftain in charge of ceremonies. The chieftain was a man, of course. In every village, the work was always divided the same way. Men took care of the fishing and the ceremonies. Mothers took care of the gardens and the children. Independent women did the trading and made most of the goods that were traded. There were a few women-men, who lived like the independent women. But they were comparatively rare. In some villages, they were thought to be perverted.

The chieftain in charge of ceremonies was on his veranda, sitting cross-legged and smoking a pipe. He was tiny and withered with a dark green complexion.

"Good day, grandfather." Vusai sat down.

"If you had my rheumatism, you wouldn't say this day is good. I can barely move! How I hate the rainy season!"

"I have come for a ceremony."

He stared at her. His eyes were black with a little yellow showing around the edges. "You are dissatisfied."

"Do I show it?"

"A little. I have also heard how you are behaving. You are rude and self-preoccupied. You break pots. You shout at children. You have come to me just in time. Help me up. As soon as we've agreed on a fee, I'll get the steam house ready."

She helped him up. They went inside and argued about the fee. He won. After that he hobbled out to the steam house. She drank tea with his wife. Only the mother in his family was still alive. She was as tiny and as withered as her husband.

"A ceremony of discontent, eh? He tried to make me go through one after my last child was born. I said, 'Leave me alone! I'm just in a bad mood. Strong tea and exercise will cure me.' And it did. But not all people are the same. For all I know, you really need his mumbo jumbo."

"Yes, grandmother."

He came back and told her the steam house was ready. She undressed and went into it. All morning she sat and sweated. He was outside, ringing a bell and singing:

"This person asks
for single-mindedness.

"This person asks
for a soul that leans
in one direction
only."

At last, when she was dizzy from the heat, he said.
"Come out."

She ran down the bank and jumped into the river.
The water was cold. "Ai!" she shouted. She dove under
water, then surfaced and swam to the middle of the
river. It was raining harder than before. She felt angry
again. She hated this time of year. The sky was always
cloudy, and the rain almost never stopped.

"Come back!" the chieftain called.

The current was taking her away from him. She
swam back to shore, then walked along the bank till
she reached him.

"Now you are purified. Go to the house of isolation. I will bring you water and the kind of tobacco
that makes people see things. Stay in the house and
smoke until something happens that makes you understand your situation. I will come by once a day and
make a lot of noise."

Vusai said, "All right."

She went to the house, walking naked through the
village. People looked away from her. It was never
polite to stare at someone who was in the middle of
a ceremony.

The house of isolation was on a hill at one end of the village, all by itself. It was small and windowless. There was a leak in the roof. Rain dripped in, and the floor was wet. This was going to be terrible, Vusai thought.

The first day nothing much happened. The rain stopped. She got hungry and thirsty. The chieftain didn't come till late in the afternoon. He rang his bell and sang:

"Whoever is responsible
for this situation—
listen to me!

"Whoever is responsible
for this situation—
give this person
some help!"

"Water!" shouted Vusai.

"Be quiet! You can have the water when I'm done singing."

He went on singing till the sun was almost down. Then he left. She heard him go down the hill, ringing his bell. She opened the door and brought in the water. She had made the pot. It was round and fat with a long neck. The glaze was black with streaks of red-dish-brown. She drank some of the water, then sighed. "The old fool! I thought he would never stop!" She looked outside again. There was a pipe on the ground. It was a long one, made of green stone. Next to the pipe was a pouch of tobacco.

"Tomorrow," she said. "I will smoke tomorrow."

The next day she was even hungrier. She began to smoke the pipe. After a while, her mother came to visit her. She was a fat woman with an angry expression. She had been dead for years.

"Why did you choose to be independent?" she asked Vusai. "A woman should have children."

Vusai did not reply.

On the third day she felt less hungry. She smoked more tobacco, and her father arrived. He was dead too. He had drowned. He came to her with seaweed in his hair. Water dripped from his tunic. He carried a net, rolled up.

"I have been trying to decide if it was worth it," he told her. "I have plenty of time at the bottom of the sea. There's really nothing else to do, except watch the fish. And I can't catch them any more, so it makes me angry to see them—so fat, so lovely, darting right above me." He put the net down. Now she was able to see that fish thrashed inside it. The strands of the net grew thin like smoke and vanished. The fish flopped away.

"You see?" said her father. "I did everything the way I was supposed to. I made nets. I made songs. I caught fish. I helped to organize all the important ceremonies. What good did it do me? Now I lie at the bottom of the ocean. The tongue is gone out of my mouth, and I don't even have a real net anymore. Only a dream net, that won't hold fish. What was the point of my life?"

"I can't tell you," said Vusai. "I don't know."

Her father vanished.

On the fourth day she saw Mawl and Shaitu. It was early in the morning. The sun was out, a rare thing this time of year. A beam of sunlight came in through the hole in the roof. It touched Mawl right in the middle of his back. He was on top of Shaitu, having sex with her. She lay on her back on the floor, looking happy. Vusai watched curiously. It must be so much easier—to do it without worrying about making children. Independent women rarely had children, of course. From the time of puberty they ate a special diet and drank tea made from the root of the plant that prevents children. This kept them safe, most of the time. But every once in a while, an independent woman got pregnant. This caused terrible problems. It had happened to an aunt of hers. The poor woman was a trader and had been planning to go on a year-long trip, Instead she stayed home and moped. After the child was born, she gave it to the mother in her family. Then she got a divorce. The child got on her nerves, she said. She didn't want to be in the same house with it. She moved to another village and remarried. The child died young of a coughing sickness.

A sad story, Vusai thought. Why did she remember it? By this time, Mawl and Shaitu were gone. She smoked another pipe of tobacco. Now she saw people with the heads of animals. They came in the door, one after another. They spoke to her loudly. She couldn't understand a word they said.

"This is bad! This is frightening! Why is this happening to me?" She threw the pipe down and covered her face with her hands. The animal-people went away.

After a while, she heard the chieftain, ringing his bell outside the house of isolation.

"I want to come out!" she called.

"Have you had a good dream?"

"No. All the dreams I've had were bad ones."

"Then keep trying." He rang the bell again.

"I want to go home!"

"You can't go home. Shut up and dream."

On the fifth day her father came back. He was still wet. There was still seaweed in his hair. But his net was gone. He said, "I wish I had become a woman-man. I would have gone traveling—not over the water, but up into the mountains. Like my second wife. I remember how she looked, so tall and strong, with a basket on her back and a long staff in her hand. Why don't you do that?"

"I don't want to."

He looked angry. "I think you are afraid to travel. Remember, someday you will be dead like me." He disappeared. She broke the pipe in two and stood up. She was a little dizzy. She stood for a moment, breathing slowly and evenly. The dizziness went away. She opened the door and went outside. As usual, it was raining. This time it was a downpour. Rivulets of water ran down the hill. "Enough is enough! I am going home!" She went toward the village, slipping and sliding in the mud. What a hateful time of year!

There was a person next to her, she noticed. He had the head of a bird. "Remember," he told her. "Without rain there is no spring. Without spring, there is no harvest. Most things have a purpose."

"Who are you?"

"A dream spirit. The effect of the tobacco hasn't worn off, though it will soon. Why did you leave the house of isolation?"

"I'm hungry, and I don't like the dreams I've been having."

"Well, I am a good dream, and my advice to you is this—go to the wife of the chieftain in charge of ceremonies. She is a wise old biddy. Ask her what she did when she felt unhappy with her life. Her husband isn't home at present. He's down at the edge of the ocean, singing over a new fishing boat. Hurry up! He will be done soon." The bird-man began to change, growing thin and changing color. Now he was yellow instead of green. He was no longer human. Instead he was a bird. He stared at her, then squawked and stalked away.

She thought for a moment, then said, "What harm can it do?"

She went to the house of the chieftain in charge of ceremonies. His wife was inside, sitting by the fire. She had a blanket around her. It was thick and brown with a pattern of knots and tufts. Local work. It wasn't as fine as the weaving done in Hui.

"Come in," the old woman said. "Sit down. Have a cup of tea."

Vusai sat down. The old woman poured tea. It was the mild kind, that relaxed the body and filled the mind with peace—for a while, at least. Vusai drank.

"Why are you here?" the old woman asked.

"My dreams told me nothing."

"Ah! So the mumbo jumbo didn't work. Well, not everyone is credulous."

"Tell me what you did when you were full of doubt."

"I told you before. I drank strong tea. I worked in my garden. And I thought about the old stories my mother told me. Old stories are full of truth. That being so, I am going to tell you a story—about how the plant that prevents children was found."

"I know the story."

The old woman looked angry. "Shut up and listen."

"Yes, grandmother."

"Long ago, there was a time when we didn't have the plant that prevents children. Every woman was a mother. Every man had a house full of children to take care of. There were no travelers and no people who worked full time at perfecting a skill. Maybe this was good, and maybe it was bad. I don't know.

"In any case, there was a woman named Ashotai. She didn't want to be a mother, and she heard about the plant that prevents children. It grew in one place in the world: on top of a very high mountain, which was overgrown with brambles and guarded by monsters. The monsters had wings and large mouths, full of venomous teeth.

"Ashotai was brave. Off she went. She got up the mountain. I used to know how, but I've forgotten. On top of the mountain, she met a spirit. The spirit said, 'Well, you made it! Good work! But are you wise as well as brave? I have a final test for you. There are two plants here. One is the plant you seek. The other is a ringer. You can take one—only one—with you. Make your choice.'

"Ashotai looked at the plants. They were exactly alike. Then she smelled the flowers on the plants. One plant had sweet flowers. The blossoms on the other plant had a sour aroma. Finally, she broke off leaves and tasted them. The plant with the sweet flowers had a wonderful taste, light and sweet like fruit. The plant with the sour aroma had a terrible taste. It was both sour and bitter.

Ashotai sat down and thought. Finally she said, 'The plant I seek will give people the ability to choose. And every real choice is bitter. If you choose to do one thing, then you lose the chance to do other things that may be just as pleasant or interesting. Because of this, it can be said—in every choice is the seed of regret, like the sour pit or core of a fruit. I think the bitter plant is the one I seek.'

"'Well, well,' said the spirit. 'You are wise. The plant you have chosen is the one that prevents children. And, as you say, every real choice is bitter. The other plant—the sweet one—is the plant that gives true peace of mind. If you had taken it, you and your people would have been happy forever. But you can't have everything. Take your plant and go.'

"So Ashotai came down from the mountain and gave the plant to her people. After that, every girl could choose whether or not to be a mother. And it was decided to give men a choice, out of fairness. Most men chose to be fathers. But a few become women-men. They act like the independent women in almost every way, and a man can take one of these into his house as a second wife."

"I know all this," said Vusai. The old woman frowned. "No you don't. You have heard the story, but you don't understand it. Remember, every choice is bitter. In every choice is the seed of regret. Well, you have eaten the fruit, Vusai. And now you are biting down on the seed. When I was your age, I realized—I was what I was. I had six children to care for and a garden and a flock of birds. I would never be a traveler. I would never have a skill as fine as the one you have. Ah! How that hurt! But I pulled weeds and drank strong tea. In time I felt better. I advise you to go back to making pots. Eat well. Sleep well. Drink medicinal teas. Your mood will improve."

Vusai put down her cup. "Is every choice a trap?"

"No." All at once the old woman had a face like a prowler from the hills. Her ears were huge and pointed. Her eyes were green, and she had a muzzle covered with yellow fur. "A choice is a path. No one can walk down two paths at one time. And when you are far enough down one path, you cannot turn around. You are too old. You do not have the time to go back to where you started." The prowler stared at her. "Pay attention to what I tell you! Remember what I say! I cannot talk to you any longer. You are almost sober. Wake up and go home. This ceremony is over."

Vusai opened her eyes. She was in the house of isolation. Rain was dripping down on her through the hole in the roof. Light shone in through the cracks around the door. She could see the dream pipe in front of her. The stem was broken.

"Ah!" said Vusai. She got up and rubbed her legs. They were stiff and sore. Then she stretched and yawned. Finally she went home.

The Warlord
of Saturn's Moons

Here I am, a silver-haired maiden lady of thirty-five, a feeder of stray cats, a window-ledge gardener, well on my way to the African violet and antimacassar stage. I can see myself at fifty, fat and a little crazy, making cucumber sandwiches for tea, and I view my future with mixed feelings. Whatever became of my childhood ambitions: joining the space patrol; winning a gold medal at the Olympics; climbing Mount Everest alone in my bathing suit, sustained only by my indomitable will and strange psychic arts learned from Hindu mystics? The saddest words of tongue or pen are something-or-other what might have been, I think. I light up a cigar and settle down to write another chapter of *The Warlord of Saturn's Moons*. A filthy habit, you say, though I'm not sure if you're referring to smoking cigars or writing science fiction. True, I reply, but both activities are pleasurable, and we maiden ladies lead lives that are notoriously short on pleasure.

So back I go to the domes of Titan and my red-headed heroine deathraying down the warlord's minions. Ah, the smell of burning flesh, the spectacle of blackened bodies collapsing. Even on paper it gets a lot of hostility out of you, so that your nights aren't troubled by dreams of murder. Terribly unrestful, those midnight slaughters and waking shaking in the darkness, your hands still feeling pressure from grabbing the victim or fighting off the murderer.

Another escape! In a power-sledge, my heroine races across Titan's methane snow, and I go and make myself tea. There's a paper on the kitchen table, waiting to tell me all about yesterday's arsons, rapes, and bloody murders. Quickly I stuff it into the garbage pail. Outside, the sky is hazy. Another high-pollution day, I think. I can see incinerator smoke rising from the apartment building across the street, which means there's no air alert yet. Unless, of course, they're breaking the law over there.

I fling open a cabinet and survey the array of teas. Earl Grey? I ponder, or Assam? Gunpowder? Jasmine? Gen Mai Cha? Or possibly an herb tea: sassafras, mint, Irish moss, or mu. Deciding on Assam, I put water on, then go back to write an exciting chase through the icy Titanian mountains. A pursuer's sledge goes over a precipice and, as my heroine hears his long shriek on her radio, my tea kettle starts shrieking. I hurry into the kitchen. Now I go through the tea-making ceremony: pouring boiling water into the pot, sloshing the water around and pouring it out, measuring the tea in, pouring more boiling water on top of the tea. All the while my mind is with my heroine, smiling grimly as she pilots the power-sledge between bare cliffs. Above her in the dark sky is the huge crescent of Saturn, a shining white line slashing across it—the famous Rings. While the tea steeps, I wipe off the counter and wash a couple of mugs. I resist a sudden impulse to pull the newspaper out from among the used tea leaves and orange peelings. I already know what's in it. The Detroit murder count will exceed 1,000 again this year; the war in Thailand is going strong; most of Europe is out on strike. I'm far better off on Titan with my heroine, who is better able to deal with her problems than I am to deal with mine. A deadly shot, she has also learned strange psychic arts from Hindu mystics, which give her great strength, endurance, mental alertness, and a naturally pleasant body odor. I wipe my hands and look at them, noticing the bitten fingernails, the torn cuticles. My heroine's long, slender, strong hands have two-inch nails filed to a point and covered with a plastic paint that makes them virtually unbreakable. When necessary, she uses them as claws. Her cuticles, of course, are in perfect condition.

I pour myself a cup of tea and return to the story. Now my heroine is heading for the mountain hideout where her partner waits: a tall, thin, dour fellow with one shining steel prosthetic hand. She doesn't know his name and she suspects he himself may have forgotten it. He insists on being called 409, his number on the prison asteroid from which he has escaped. She drives as quickly as she dares, thinking of his long face, burned almost black by years of strong radiation on Mars and in space, so the white webbing of scars on its right side show up clearly. His eyes are grey, so pale they seem almost colorless. As I write about 409, I find myself stirred by the same passion that stirs my heroine. I begin to feel uneasy, so I stop and drink some tea. I can see I'm going to have trouble with 409. It's never wise to get too involved with one's characters. Besides, I'm not his type. I imagine the way he'd look at me, indifference evident on his dark, scarred face. I could, of course, kill him off. My heroine would then spend the rest of the story avenging him, though she'd never get to the real murderer—me. But this solution, while popular among writers, is unfair.

I go into the kitchen, extract a carrot from a bunch in the icebox, clean it, and eat it. After that, I write the heroine's reunion with 409. Neither of them is demonstrative. They greet each other with apparent indifference and retire to bed. I skip the next scene. How can I watch that red-headed hussy in bed with the man I'm beginning to love?

I continue the story at the moment when their alarm bell rings, and they awake to find the warlord's rocket planes have landed all around their hideout. A desperate situation! 409 suggests that he make a run for it in their rocket plane. While the warlord's minions pursue him, my heroine can sneak away in the power-sledge. The plan has little chance of success, but they can think of none better. They bid farewell to one another, and my heroine goes to wait in the sledge for the signal telling her 409 has taken off. As she waits, smoking a cigar, she thinks of what little she knows about 409. He was a fighter pilot in the war against the Martian colony and was shot down and captured. While in prison something happened to him that he either can't remember or refuses to talk about, and, when the war ended and he was released, he became a criminal. As for herself, she had been an ordinary sharpshooter and student of Hindu mysticism, a follower of Swami

Bluestone of the Brooklyn Vedic Temple and Rifle Range. Then she discovered by accident the warlord's plot to overthrow the government of Titan, the only one of Saturn's satellites not under his control. With her information about the plot, the government may still be saved. She has to get to Titan City with the microfilm dot!

The alarm bell rings, and she feels the ground shake as 409's plane takes off. Unfortunately I'm writing the story from my heroine's point of view. I want to describe 409 blasting off, the warlord's rocket planes taking off after him, chasing him as he flies through the narrow, twisting valleys, the planes' rockets flaring red in the valley shadows and missiles exploding into yellow fireballs. All through this, of course, 409's scarred face remains tranquil, and his hands move quickly and surely over the plane's controls. His steel prosthetic hand gleams in the dim light from the dials. But I can't put this in the story, since my heroine sees none of it as she slides off in the opposite direction, down a narrow trail hidden by overhanging cliffs.

I am beginning to feel tense, I don't know why. Possibly 409's dilemma is disturbing me. He's certainly in danger. In any case, my tea is cold. I turn on the radio, hoping for some relaxing rock music and go to get more tea. But it's twenty to the hour, time for the news, and I get the weekend body count: two men found dead in suspected westside dope house, naked body of woman dragged out of Detroit River. I hurry back and switch to a country music station. On it, someone's singing about how he intends to leave the big city and go back down south. As I go back into the kitchen, I think:

Carry me back to Titan.
That's where I want to be.
I want to repose
On the methane snows
At the edge of a frozen sea.

I pour out the old tea and refill the cup with tea that's hot. The radio begins to make that awful beepity-beep-beepity sound that warns you the news is coming up. I switch back to the rock station, where the news is now over. I'm safe for another fifty-five minutes, unless there's a special news flash to announce a five-car pile-up or an especially ghastly murder.

The plan works! For my heroine, at least. She doesn't know yet if 409 got away. She speeds off unpursued. The power-sledge's heating system doesn't quite keep her warm, and the landscape around her is forbidding: bare cliffs and narrow valleys full of methane snow, overhead the dark blue sky. Saturn has set, and the tiny sun is rising, though she can't see it yet. On the high mountains the ice fields begin to glitter with its light. On she races, remembering how she met 409 in the slums of The Cup on Ganymede, as she fled the warlord's assassins. She remembers being cornered with no hope of escape. Then behind the two assassins a tall figure appeared, and the shining steel hand smashed down on the back of one assassin's head. As the other assassin turned, he got the hand across his face. A moment or two more, and both the assassins were on the ground, unconscious. Then she saw 409's twisted grin for the first time and his colorless eyes appraising her.

There I go, I think, getting all heated up over 409. The radio is beginning to bother me, so I shut it off and re-light my cigar. I find myself wishing that men like 409 really existed. Increasingly in recent years, I've found real men boring. Is it possible, as some scientists argue, that the Y chromosome produces an inferior human being? There certainly seem to be far fewer interesting men than interesting women. But theories arguing that one kind of human being is naturally inferior make me anxious. I feel my throat muscles tightening and the familiar tense, numb feeling spreading across my face and my upper back. Quickly I return to my story.

Now out on the snowy plain, my heroine can see the transparent domes of Titan City ahead of her, shining in the pale sunlight. Inside the domes the famous pastel towers rise, their windows reflecting the sun. Her power-sledge speeds down the road, through the drifts that half cover it. Snow sprays up on either side of the sledge, so my heroine has trouble seeing to the left and right. As a result, it's some time before she sees the power-sledges coming up behind her on the right. At the same moment that she looks over and sees them, their sleek silver bodies shining in the sunlight and snow-sprays shooting up around them, her radio begins to go beep-beep-beep. She flicks it on. The voice of Janos Black, the warlord's chief agent on Titan, harsh and slurred by a thick Martian accent, tells her the bad news: 409's plane has been shot down. He ejected before it crashed. Even now the warlord's men are going after the ejection capsule, which is high on a cliff, wedged between a rock spire and the cliff wall. Janos offers her a trade: 409 for the microdot. But Janos may well be lying; 409 may have gotten away or else been blown up. She feels a sudden constriction of her throat at the thought of 409 dead. She flicks off the radio and pushes the power-sledge up to top speed. She realizes as she does so that 409 is unlikely to fare well if Janos gets ahold of him. Janos' wife and children died of thirst after the great Martian network of pipelines was blown apart by Earther bombs, and Janos knows that 409 was a pilot in the Earther expeditionary force.

I write another exciting chase, this one across the snowy plain toward the pink, green, blue, and yellow towers of Titan City. The warlord's power-sledges are gaining. Their rockets hit all around my heroine's sledge, and fire and black smoke erupt out of the snow. Swearing in a low monotone, she swings the sledge back and forth in a zig-zag evasive pattern.

I stop to puff on my cigar and discover it's gone out again. My tea is cold. But the story's beginning at last to interest me. I keep on writing.

As my heroine approaches the entrance to Titan City, she's still a short distance ahead of her pursuers. Her radio beeps. It's Janos Black again. He tells her his men have gotten to the ejection capsule and are lowering it down the cliff. Any minute now, they'll have it down where they can open it and get 409 out.

Ignoring Janos, she concentrates on slowing her sledge and bringing it through the city's outer gate into the airlock. A moment or two later, she's safe. But what about 409?

Frankly, I don't know. I stand and stretch, decide to take a bath, and go to turn the water on. The air pollution must be worse than I originally thought. I have the dopey feeling I get on the days when the pollution is really bad. I look out the window. Dark grey smoke is still coming out of the chimneys across the street. Maybe I should call the Air Control number (dial AIR-CARE) and complain. But it takes a peculiar kind of person to keep on being public-spirited after it becomes obvious it's futile. I decide to put off calling Air Control and water my plants instead. Every bit of oxygen helps, I think. I check the bathtub—it's not yet half-full—and go back to writing. After a couple of transitional paragraphs, my heroine finds herself in the antechamber to the Titan Council's meeting room. There is a man there, standing with his back to her. He's tall and slender, and his long hair is a shade between blond and grey. He turns and she recognizes the pale, delicate-looking face. This is Michael Stelladoro, the warlord of Saturn's moons. His eyes, she notices, are as blue as cornflowers, and he has a delightful smile. He congratulates her on escaping his power-sledges, then tells her that his men have gotten 409 out of the ejection capsule. He is still alive and as far as they can determine uninjured. They have given 409 a shot of Sophamine. At this my heroine gasps with horror. Sophamine, she knows, is an extremely powerful tranquilizer used to control schizophrenia. One dose is enough to make most people dependent on it, and withdrawal takes the form of a nightmarish psychotic fugue. The warlord smiles his delightful smile and turns on the radio he has clipped to his belt. A moment later my heroine hears 409's voice telling her that he has in fact been captured. He sounds calm and completely uninterested in his situation. That, she knows, is the Sophamine. It hasn't affected his perception of reality. He knows where he is and what is likely to happen to him, but he simply doesn't care. When the Sophamine wears off, all the suppressed emotions will well up, so intense that the only way he'll be able to deal with them will be to go insane, temporarily at least.

The warlord tells her he regrets having to use the Sophamine, but he was certain that 409 would refuse to talk unless he was either drugged or tortured, and there simply wasn't enough time to torture him.

"You fiend!" my heroine cries.

The warlord smiles again, as delightfully as before, and says if she gives the microdot to the Titan Council, he will turn 409 over to Janos Black who will attempt to avenge on him all the atrocities committed by the Earthers on Mars.

What can she do? As she wonders, the door to the meeting room opens, and she is asked to come in. For a moment, she thinks of asking the Titanians to arrest the warlord. Almost as if he's read her mind, he tells her there's no point in asking the Titanians to arrest him. He has diplomatic immunity and a warfleet waiting for him to return.

She turns to go into the meeting room. "I'll tell Janos the good news," the warlord says softly and turns his radio on.

She hesitates, then thinks, a man this evil must be stopped, no matter what the cost. She goes into the meeting room.

I remember the bath water, leap up, and run into the bathroom. The tub is brim-full and about to overflow. I turn off the tap, let out some of the water, and start to undress. After I climb into the tub, I wonder how I'm going to get 409 out of the mess he's in. Something will occur to me. I grab the bar of soap floating past my right knee.

After bathing, I put on a pink and silver muumuu and make a fresh pot of tea. Cleanliness is next to godliness, I think as I sit down to write.

My heroine tells her story to the Titan Council and produces the microdot. On it is the warlord's plan for taking over the government of Titan and a list of all the Titanian officials he has subverted. The president of the council thanks her kindly and tells her that they already have a copy of the microdot, obtained for them by an agent of theirs who has infiltrated the warlord's organization. "Oh no! Oh no!" my heroine cries. Startled, the president asks her what's wrong. She explains that she has sacrificed her partner, her love to bring them the information they already had. "Rest easy," the president says. "Our agent is none other than Janos Black. He won't harm 409."

Thinking of Janos' family dying of thirst in an isolated settlement, my heroine feels none too sure of this. But there's nothing left for her to do except hope.

After that, I describe her waiting in Titan City for news of 409, wandering restlessly through the famous gardens, barely noticing the beds of Martian sandflowers, the blossoming magnolia trees, the pools of enormous silver carp. Since the warlord now knows that the Titan Council knows about his schemes, the council moves quickly to arrest the officials he's subverted. The newscasts are full of scandalous revelations, and the warlord leaves Titan for his home base on Tethys, another one of Saturn's moons. My heroine pays no attention to the newscasts or to the excited conversations going on all around her. She thinks of the trip she and 409 made from Ganymede to Titan in a stolen moon-hopper, remembering 409's hands on the ship's controls, the way he moved in zero-G, his colorless eyes and his infrequent, twisted smile. Cornball, I think, but leave the passage in. I enjoy thinking about 409 as much as my heroine does.

After two days, Janos Black arrives in a police plane. 409 is with him. Janos comes to see my heroine to bring her the news of their arrival. He's a tall man with a broad chest and spindly arms and legs. His face is ruddy and Slavic, and his hair is prematurely white. He tells her that he kept 409 prisoner in the warlord's secret headquarters in the Titanian mountains till the Titanian police moved in and arrested everybody.

"Then he's all right," she cries joyfully.

Janos shakes his head.

"Why not?"

"The Sophamine," Janos explains. "When it wore off, he got hit with the full force of all his repressed feelings, especially, I think, the feelings he had about the war on Mars. Think of all that anger and terror and horror and guilt flooding into his conscious mind. He tried to kill himself. We stopped him, and he almost killed a couple of us in the process. By we I mean myself and the warlord's men; this happened before the police moved in. We had to give him another shot of

Sophamine. He's still full of the stuff. From what I've heard, the doctors want to keep giving it to him. They think the first shot of Sophamine he got destroyed his old system of dealing with his more dangerous emotions, which are now overwhelming him. The doctors say on Sophamine he can function more or less normally. Off it, they think he'll be permanently insane."

"You planned this!" she cries. Janos shakes his head. "The warlord gave the order, miss. I only obeyed it. But I didn't mind this time. I didn't mind."

I stop to drink some tea. Then I write the final scene in the chapter: my heroine's meeting with 409. He's waiting for her in a room at the Titan City Hospital. The room is dark. He sits by the window looking out at the tall towers blazing with light and at the dome above them, which reflects the towers' light so it's impossible to look through it at the sky. She can see his dark shape and the red tip of the cigar he smokes.

"Do you mind if I turn on the lights?" she asks.

"No."

She finds the button and presses it. The ceiling begins to glow. She looks at 409. He lounges in his chair, his feet up on a table. She realizes it's the first time she's seen him look really relaxed. Before this, he's always seemed tense, even when asleep.

"How are you?" she asks.

"Fine." His voice sounds tranquil and indifferent. She can't think of anything to say. He looks at her, his dark, scarred face expressionless. Finally he says, "Don't let it bother you. I feel fine." He pauses. She still can't think of anything to say. He continues. "The pigs don't want me for anything here on Titan. I think I'll be able to stay."

"What're you going to do here?"

"Work, I guess. The doctors say I can hold down a job if I keep taking Sophamine." He draws on the cigar, so the tip glows red, then blows out the smoke. He's looking away from her at the towers outside the window. She begins weeping. He looks back at her. "I'm all right. Believe me, I feel fine."

But she can't stop weeping.

Enough for today, I think and put down my pencil. Tomorrow, I'll figure out a way to get 409 off Sophamine. Where there's life there's hope and so forth, I tell myself.

The Lovers

There was a woman of the Ahara. She came of a good line within the lineage[1] and grew up to be tall and broad with thick, glossy fur. Her eyes were pale grey, an unusual color in that part of the world. From childhood on, her nickname was Eyes-of-crystal. If she had a fault, it lay in her personality. She was bit too fierce and solitary.

Her home was in the town of Ahara Tsal, which stood on top of the Tsal River bluffs. To the west and south lay the farms and pastures of her lineage: a flat rich land. To the north and east was the river valley, wide and marshy and full of animals. Eyes-of-crystal liked to go down there into the wilderness and ride and hunt. Her mother warned her this was dangerous.

"You'll get strange ideas and possibly meet things and people you don't want to meet."

But Eyes-of-crystal refused to listen.

Don't think this is a story about how she met ghosts or bandits or some horrible great animal like a *ulkuwa* and learned that her mother was right and she ought to have stayed at home. That's another story entirely, and maybe a good one. But the pain that Eyes-of-crystal

1 Literally "of a good thread within the woven cord."

46

encountered did not come from disobedience, and it did not come to her when she was away from home.

As mentioned before, she grew up to be large and strong. When she was twenty-five, her relatives decided to breed her. At this time, the Ahara were the second most powerful lineage in the world, and this young woman came from a line that produced really fine children. The Ahara wanted to breed her with someone important. They looked around, and who did they see? Eh Manhata, who was the greatest warrior of the age. His lineage, the Eh, stood in front of everyone else. They had no equal. Only the Ahara came close. So the young woman's relatives entered into negotiations with the senior women of Eh.

Eyes-of-crystal knew about this, but paid as little attention as possible. She had never wanted to be a mother, but she had always known that she had no choice. At times, she wished that she had come from a less excellent line. If only there had been something wrong or unhealthy about her immediate family! Maybe then she would have been left alone. But her brothers and male first cousins were sturdy fighters. Her sisters and female first cousins were producing babies like furry butter balls. Every relative was co-operative, moral, intelligent, and well-put-together.

What a curse, thought Eyes-of-crystal and went back down to the river to hunt. There, in the dark forest of the flood plain, she found a kind of peace. Often, she found animals as well and brought them home, dead and bloody, across the back of her well-trained *tsin*. Imagine her as a kind of Diana, a grey-furred virgin huntress, about to lose everything she valued.

After a while, her mother called her in for a conference. One of her uncles was there as well, her mother's full brother, a soldier of middle age with a great scar across his face and one eye missing.

"You know that we have been speaking with the Eh," her mother said. "We wanted Eh Manhata as the father of your child."

"Yes," said Eyes-of-crystal. "I know this."

"He is not available," her mother said. "According to the Eh, they can't afford to take him out of the current war and send him here."

"There may be more going on than we can see," her uncle added. "I have never heard of Eh Manhata fathering any children, even in those periods when the war has slowed down."

Her mother's head tilted in the gesture that can mean either agreement or consideration. "There are men, even great men, who are not able to father children for one reason or another."

Eye-of-crystal knew the reasons, of course. The People do not enjoy thinking about the unpleasant aspects of life, any more than humans do. But if a thing is unavoidable, then it must be looked at, and they have never misled their children about what was involved in producing the next generation. Some men were infertile, and others were impotent. These were physical problems and comparatively rare. The most common problem was one that humans would call psychological, and the People would say was moral or spiritual. There were men who simply could not overcome their natural aversion to sex with women. They were fine with other men, but put them in a breeding situation and nothing happened.[2]

"They have offered us Manhata's full brother," her mother said. "He has fathered a number of children, and most of them look good. Your uncle has met him, which is why I asked him to be present at this conference."

"They are twins," her uncle said. "When they came out into the world, Manhata was already bigger and stronger. He has always been quicker and more forceful than his brother. There are people who say he took something from his brother in the womb. I wouldn't be surprised."

"This doesn't sound promising," Eyes-of-crystal said.

"There's nothing wrong with Eh Shawin. He looks very much like Eh Manhata, though he isn't as tall or broad, and something is missing, as I said before. Manhata is like a man in sunlight. No one can overlook him. Shawin is a man at the edge of a forest, in shadow and not entirely visible. But he's a good soldier, and no one has ever questioned his courage or intelligence. And he is Eh Manhata's only full brother."

"No mating can tie us closer to Eh than this one," her mother said. "And no lineage is more important to us. If we're lucky, some of Manhata's qualities will show up in your child or children."

"You want me to do this," Eyes-of-crystal said.

Her mother said, "Yes."

She agreed. A message was sent to Eh. Eyes-of-crystal took her bow and went down along the river to shoot birds.

---

2 Literally "nothing came forward." The *double entendre* is in the original.

This happened in the late spring. Eh Shawin did not arrive until mid-summer. He came alone, which was not surprising. The road from Eh to Ahara was usually safe, and his brother was leading a campaign in the north against the Alliance of the Five Less One. All his male relatives would be there. In peaceful times, of course, they would have ridden with him and made rude jokes about heterosexuality. It was always the job of one's own male relatives to demoralize, while the men of the other lineage were required to be friendly and encouraging.

In any case, Shawin appeared alone at the gate of Ahara Tsal. The guards asked him to wait and sent a messenger ahead. There was time for her family to gather in the courtyard of their great house: her mother, her aunt, the older female cousins, and the two men who were not at war.

Eyes-of-crystal was on a balcony. There were rules and courtesies in a proper mating. One does not meet the man right off. But there was nothing wrong in watching, as she did.

He rode in. His animal was dusty and tired, but had a good shape with powerful haunches and shoulders and a wide head that might indicate intelligence. It was solid brown, a rare and expensive color.

The man was as dusty as the *tsin* and dressed like an ordinary soldier. But he swung down gracefully, and once he was on the ground she could see he was tall, standing eye to eye with her mother and looming over the two old men, as they came forward to welcome him.

All the rituals of greeting were performed. It seemed to her that Shawin moved through them with unusual precision and grace, like the traveling actors she had seen now and then. They came to Ahara Tsal and set up their stage in the main square. There they danced and told the stories of heroes. It occurred to her as a child that she wanted to be two things: a soldier or an actor. Both were impossible.

One of her sisters was on the balcony with Eyes-of-crystal. She looked down at the man in the courtyard and said, "He isn't much to look at, is he?"

Eyes-of-crystal held her tongue, though there was plenty she could have said. The sister had mated for the first time with a son of Merin, a beautiful man who liked fine clothing and jewelry. His eyes had been blue-green, the color of malachite. His manners had been good enough, especially at first. But it had taken her sister a long time to get pregnant, and the man became obviously restless. He was anxious to get back to the war and to his lover, the men of Ahara said. When he learned that the sister was finally pregnant, he let out a shout of joy, and he left as soon as he decently could.

Eyes-of-crystal mentioned none of this. For one thing, the sister was still pregnant and with twins, if her size was any indication. Discomfort had ruined the woman's usually good disposition, and it was never a good idea to criticize the father of an unborn child.

Eyes-of-crystal kept her lips firmly closed over the *hwarhath* proverb which means, "handsome is as handsome does."

The next day she was introduced to the man. He'd taken a bath and put on a new kilt, covered with embroidery. The grip of his sword was white bone bound with rings of gold. His fur was brushed and glossy.

That was as much as she learned about him. Their meeting was formal and brief. The words they spoke to each other were set by tradition. When they had finished, her great uncles led Eh Shawin off to meet with other men. She went off with her female relatives.

For the most part, the *hwarhath* would prefer not to think about what their ancestors had to go through, before the development of artificial insemination. But the information is there if you want to look for it, and the author of this story clearly did her research.

Remember that heterosexuality was—and is—frightening to the People. In it lies the power of generation and destruction. They know—and have always known—that the survival of their species depends on keeping men and women apart. But through most of their history, the survival of their society depended on mating.

They did what humans also do, when faced with something frightening and unavoidable: death, for example, birth or marriage. They used ritual to protect the act and limit it and direct its power. They used humor and drugs to diminish their fear.

Eh Shawin spent the day with the men of Ahara, talking and getting a little drunk. Eyes-of-crystal spent the day getting ready for the night, and the author of the story describes every detail: the ritual bath, the ceremonies of protection, the comic skits performed by female cousins, the elaborate mating robe.

Most likely, there is an element of malice in all this description. "Look, look," the author is saying to her readers. "This is what you are trying to forget. This is where we came from. It's as inescapable as shit."

Finally, at nightfall, Eyes-of-crystal was led up to the mating chamber: a large circular room high in a tower. Most of the space was filled by a bed, its wooden frame elaborately carved. Two chairs stood by a window. A lamp burned on the table between them. Eyes-of-crystal sat down. Her robe was stiff with embroidery. There was no way to relax. She had been given a potion, so the bed did not frighten her. Her relatives fussed around, straightening the cover on the bed, trimming the wick on the lamp, offering good advice.

Finally, there was the sound of male voices, mostly drunk, at the bottom of the tower. The women grew silent. Eyes-of-crystal heard footsteps on the stairs: one person only, climbing steadily. The others had stayed behind, as was proper. One fellow kept shouting, "Good luck!"

A couple of the women whispered angrily. This was a serious—a sacred—business, and it ought to be carried forward with gravity. A little bit of something to drink did no harm. But men never knew when to stop. Any excuse for a drinking party!

The door opened, and there Eh Shawin was. A torch shone in back of him, so he was edged with red and yellow light. A moment later, he was in the room and standing in the shadows along the curving wall.

The women left. Several of them touched Eyes-of-crystal as they passed her, but no one spoke. There was only the rustle of clothing, the slap of sandals on the bare stone floor and the breathing of an especially large and solid aunt as she went down the winding stairs. Last to go was Eyes-of-crystal's mother.

Eh Shawin closed the door, came over and sat down in the chair across from Eyes-of-crystal. Now she was frightened, in spite of the potion. He leaned forward and looked at her, frowning. "They have drugged you."

"Yes."

He sighed. "The first night is always like this. I'm going to tell you something, Ahara Pai, though I don't know if you'll be able to understand it at the moment. Still, I believe in acting directly[3] and in saying what's in my mind.

"There are many families who want to interbreed with Eh, and all of them are interested in having my brother as a father. But as you probably know, our lineage cannot let him leave the field of battle.

"Because I'm Eh Manhata's twin, I've been sent on trips like this—" He paused. "More times than I can remember. I know far more about this situation than is usual for a man, and I have formed my own opinions about how to go about producing children."

Eyes-of-crystal would have been shocked, if she had been sober. Thanks to the potion, she remained calm.

"These drugs and rituals do nothing good! The woman is frightened, and the man would be, if he wasn't drunk, as he usually is. It's surprising he remembers what it is he has to do.

3   Literally "with *katiad*." This is the most important male virtue. If a man has it, he is steadfast, forthright, honest, and sincere. He travels like an arrow that is well-made and well-shot, straight to the target.

"In my opinion, everything goes best if the two people are sober and comfortable with one another. The women seems to get pregnant more quickly, and it's my impression that the child turns out better. And so I have developed my own way of doing this. I try to make it as ordinary as possible."

"Do your female relatives let you have these opinions?" asked Eyes-of crystal. "It seems odd."

He glanced up and smiled briefly. "Remember that they've known me from childhood. Eh Manhata is fierce. I am stubborn."

He changed the subject then and asked her about hunting. The men of Ahara had told him she liked to hunt. It was an unusual trait in a woman, but not wrong or shameful. His home was on the plain. He knew what it was like to chase game over flat land and along the little rivers of his country. What was the great river like for hunting?

She tried to answer him, but she was frightened, and the drug made it hard for her to think and speak. Her mind kept coming back to the present situation, though with decreasing fear. For one thing, his questions were so ordinary. For another, the drug was making her sleepy. Her thoughts moved more and more slowly, like people wading through a heavy fall of snow.

"Maybe we should have this conversation another time," Eh Shawin said finally. He paused, then continued, his voice quiet and gentle. "There is one thing I have never been able to change. Your relatives and mine have expectations about what will happen tonight. We must meet those expectations.

"I can do the thing slowly and try to find some way to make it pleasant for you, or I can do it quickly and get it over."

"Quickly," said Eyes-of-crystal.

Eh Shawin inclined his head in the motion of agreement, then asked if she wanted light or darkness.

"Darkness," said Eyes-of-crystal.

He licked his fingers and put out the lamp.

The home world of the People has no moon, but the stars are brilliant, and the People have better night vision than humans. Most likely, the man and woman could see each other as they undressed. Maybe their eyes gleamed occasionally, reflecting starlight. Their dark solid bodies must certainly have been visible, as they moved past the star-filled windows or settled on the bed, which was covered with a mating blanket of bleached fabric as white as snow or bone.

The author of the story does not tell us any of this, though she describes their mating with clinical detail. Most likely, she was working from the old mating manuals, which are still available in libraries, though not (of course) in sections that children can access. There is no reason to believe that she is writing from personal experience.

After they finished, the man went to sleep. Eyes-of-crystal lay next to him, looking out a window at the sky. She could see the Banner of the Goddess, the Milky Way.

What had the Goddess been thinking of, when she devised this method for making people? It was like a great ugly knot in the net of kinship and cooperation and love that held all of them—women and men, adults and children—together. Impossible to understand!

She woke in the morning and found Eh Shawin gone, though she could see the place where he'd lain. Her body hurt. She got up groaning and went down to the women's bathroom. There was hot water ready and a cousin to help her.

Hah! It was good to wash and then to soak in a tub of clean water scented with herbs. The cousin was middle aged, but had never been bred. One of her feet was twisted. It had been that way from birth, and this was not a trait the Ahara wanted continued. She barely spoke to Eyes-of-crystal, either out of envy or embarrassment.

At last, Eyes-of-crystal got out of the tub and rubbed herself dry. The cousin brought a fresh new tunic. She put it on. Her female relatives would be waiting for her in the eating room and the kitchen. She had no wish to see them. Eyes-of-crystal thanked her cousin and went out to the stables.

Light slanted in the little high windows. The air smelled of hay and *tsina*. Most of the stalls were empty, the animals gone to war. But a few remained: the mares and geldings that children rode and her own hunters. She went to look at her favorite, a blue-grey stallion. His legs and hind quarters had white stripes, and his horns were as black as obsidian.

Eh Shawin stood at the end of the stall. "A fine animal," he said. "What do you call him?"

"Direct Action."

"A good name. I talked to your mother this morning and explained that I don't want to inconvenience your male relatives. There are so few home at present, and most are so old! They don't have the energy to be entertaining a guest. And I do best in these situations if I keep regular hours and maintain my ordinary habits. So—" He glanced up briefly and smiled. "Your mother has agreed that it makes better sense for me to go out riding with you. I get the exercise I need, and the old men of Ahara get their rest."

It wasn't like her mother to agree to anything un-usual, but Shawin was clever and plausible. There are men who know how to charm women, just as there are men who know how to charm men. These two quali-ties don't usually come together in one person.

Eyes-of-crystal had the impression that Eh Shawin was no exception to this rule. Her male relatives did not dislike the man, but it wasn't likely they'd go out of the way for him.

"My *tsin* hasn't recovered from our journey as yet, but one of your cousins has offered me this animal." He led her to another stall.

She knew the animal there: a large gelding. Its color was solid purple-brown.

"He told me its name is Consistent Behavior, which sounds promising, though I'm curious why an animal this color was gelded."

She knew and told him. The animal had a sullen disposition. This wasn't a problem for riding. "Unless you want to go quickly." But Consistent Behavior was no good for hunting, and the animal would have been dangerous in a war.

Eh Shawin laughed.

"My cousin meant no discourtesy. You see how little we have available." She gestured around at the empty stalls.

"I don't take offense easily. That's my brother."

They saddled and rode out. The author of this story is anonymous, but she almost certainly came from one of the lineages along the river, maybe from Ahara. Her description of the country is detailed, and it reads like a real experience, not something she got out of a book.

They went east, along a narrow trail that led past fields of *hwal* and *antim*. The sky was clear, except for a handful of high clouds, and the air smelled of dust and dry vegetation. Small bugs filled the weeds along the trail. The names of the bugs are given: sunfly, hopper, *pirig, heln,* and scarlet warrior.

Eh Shawin asked about hunting a second time.

Eyes-of-crystal told him about the many fine animals and birds to be found in the marshes along the river Tsal and in the flood plain forest.

It was obvious that he knew about hunting. The questions he asked were intelligent. But he had never spent much time around water. She told him about the giant fish that lived in the river. They were longer than a man and had teeth like knives. Their dispositions were nasty. Her people hunted them with nets and spears.

"That must be something," Eh Shawin said and then exhaled loudly. They had come to the top of the bluffs. The front of them was the river valley, wide and deep, full of many channels that wound through the forest and marshland, so the entire valley was like a belt made of strips of colored leather woven together: green, blue-green, brown, and pale red.

The two of them dismounted and let their animals graze. They spoke more about hunting. He reached over and stroked her shoulder the way a female lover might. Eyes-of-crystal frowned. After a moment he took his hand away and leaned back till he was lying full-length on the stony ground, his hands forming a resting place for his head.

Now she was made uneasy by his silence. "What is your brother like?" she asked.

He glanced at her. In the bright sunlight, his pupils had contracted to lines she could not see. His eyes were like windows onto an empty blue sky.

"That's a question I've heard before. 'Tell us about Eh Manhata, Eh Shawin.'"

"Does it make you angry to be asked?"

"No. It's always been obvious that he was something special, even when we were children. Everyone knew if he lived to be a man, he would be either a hero or a monster.

"He is fierce and without fear, commanding, strong, clever about war. No one can match him as a leader in battle. So long as he's alive, our lineage will always win.

"He loves our mother and our female relatives, and he never acts without consulting them—except on the battlefield, of course. He is loyal to Eh. He respects the Goddess."

He stopped talking. There was no noise except bugs singing in the vegetation.

"I know all this," said Eyes-of-crystal.

"Then you know Eh Manhata." The man sat up. "Let's ride more."

That day they stayed on the plain above the river. In the afternoon, they returned to Ahara Tsal. At night, they mated again in the tower room. It was as unpleasant as the first time, but she didn't lie awake for as long afterward.

The weather remained hot and dry: good late summer weather. They got in the habit of going out almost every day. Eyes-of-crystal showed the man of Eh her country: the cultivated fields, the marshes and forest. They hunted the animals available in that season, before the fall migrations began. The man was a good companion: patient, observant, respectful of her skill and knowledge, unmoved by violence and death.

She liked him, though she had never expected to like a man who was not a close relative and though he did things that made her uneasy.

One afternoon Eyes-of-crystal shot a *ral*[4] in the marshes along the river. The animal went down, but it wasn't dead. It struggled to rise, making a bleating noise. Eh Shawin was the one who dismounted and cut its throat. As he stuck his knife in, the *ral* jerked and twisted its neck. Blood spurted onto his clothing, and he made the hissing sound that indicates anger or disgust. He finished killing the *ral*, then pulled off his

4 This is a marsh-dwelling quadruped herbivore. Its body is like a small antelope or deer except for the broad three-toed feet. Its head is surprisingly large and looks as if it might belong to a refined wart hog. The males have tusks. Both sexes have little piggy eyes and large mobile ears, which are striped lavender and pale yellow inside. Their backs are dull red, almost the same color as the dominant vegetation of the marshes. Their rumps are yellow, except around the anus, where there is a circular area that is entirely hairless. The bare skin is bright pink

tunic and sank it in a pool of water. Naked, he eviscerated the animal. She had never seen an adult man without clothing. It made her uncomfortable.

She kept herself busy with the *tsina*. Her Direct Action was not troubled by the scent of blood, but the animal that Shawin was riding—a young stallion that she had not finished training yet—was fidgety. He might try to run.

When Shawin had finished, he waded into the water and washed himself, then the tunic.

"Put that on," she said when he came back to shore.

"Wet? No."

"I don't like this."

For a moment he said nothing, but concentrated on wringing out the tunic. Then he glanced up briefly. "There's no one here except the two of us, and we have been spending every night in the same bed, neither of us wearing anything. Do you really think we need to be formal?"

"Yes."

"Maybe you ought to go on ahead," Eh Shawin said. "You'll have to take the *ral*. My *tsin* isn't going to be willing to carry it."

She did as he suggested and rode home alone, troubled by the memory of him, his fur slicked down by water and his body evident. He was rangy with large bones and long muscles, narrow everywhere except through the shoulders. Made for speed rather than endurance, Eyes-of-crystal thought. In a way beautiful, though not with the sleek beauty of a woman.[5]

5 The build described here is not typical of male *hwarhath*, who tend to be solid with torsos that go straight up and

He ought to be more modest. He had not seemed especially bothered by the fact that he was naked. Maybe he had spent too much time fulfilling mating contracts. It had become ordinary for him to be around women who were not relatives and to do things with them that most men did only once or twice in their lives.

That evening, in the tower room, she asked about his behavior.

"If I hadn't washed the tunic right away, the stain would have sunk in, and I like that tunic. It's almost new, and I don't know if you noticed, but the embroidery over the shoulders is really fine. I shouldn't have worn it for hunting. I wasn't expecting to make quite so big a mess."

"Are you this way in battle?" she asked. "Fastidious?"

"No. Of course not. Though I never like it when something good is ruined: a piece of clothing, a weapon. But I don't think about that till later. In battle, there are only two things on my mind: staying alive and following my brother's orders."

There was something in his voice when he spoke about his brother that troubled her. "Do you like him?"

Eh Shawin glanced up. The room was dark except for a single lantern, flickering on the table between them, and his pupils had expanded to wide black bars. "Manhata? What a question to ask." He licked his fingers and put out the light.

One of her cousins was home from the war while an injury to his leg healed. By this time, he was starting to hobble around, and he asked Eh Shawin to practice

---

down. The author is giving us a male protagonist who is a bit odd and humanish in appearance.

fighting with him. This was something women were not supposed to watch, but Eyes-of-crystal climbed onto a roof that overlooked the fighting ground. The two men used swords, the long heavy kind that had only one purpose. No man even carried a weapon like that, unless he was going to war. Eh Shawin handled his sword with ease. He was obviously a better fighter than her cousin, and this was not due simply to her cousin's injury. He was as quick as she had expected and strong as well. Lovely to watch, the woman thought as she crouched on the roof tiles. If she had a son, this quickness and strength would be useful. If she had a daughter, maybe the child would get Eh Shawin's discipline. With luck, his oddness would not be transmitted.

Her time for bleeding came. So did the blood. She wasn't pregnant. She stayed away from him for several nights, as was customary.

"That tells me I have another 40 days here," Eh Shawin said. "I'm not sorry, though I have to say your male relatives are boring. But I like you, and my lineage does not have another breeding contract that requires me. Once you're pregnant, I'll have to rejoin the army."

"You don't like the war."

"It's been going on a long time. After a while, everything seems as if it's happened before. There are only so many ways to kill and die. Even my brother has not managed to find much that is new in those areas."

"You are very peculiar," said Eyes-of-crystal. "I hope it doesn't come out in your children."

He laughed. "No one has complained to my female relatives."

This conversation look place atop a river bluff. They ended in this place often. He shared her love of the wide river valley. The foliage was getting its autumn colors. The river was dark brown like weathered bronze, except where it reflected the forest or the sky. Everything seemed to be shifting and changing. She looked out and thought of traveling like a tree floating in the water or a bird rising on the wind.

Maybe when this over, and she was pregnant, she would go to visit another town. There were several lineages nearby that were closely tied to Ahara. She had relatives, women who had been fathered by men of her lineage. She even had a former lover, a woman of Shulnowa. They had met at a festival and visited back and forth, and then the war grew dangerous for a time, and they exchanged tokens and messages. That ended finally. But maybe she could go to Shulnowa and visit one of her minor cousins. Maybe she would meet the lover. How could she avoid it in a town that size?

Eh Shawin ran a hand down her arm, stroking the fur. "I think I'd like to have sex right now."

"Here? In the sunlight?"

"We aren't getting anywhere by having sex in the dark."

Her bleeding had stopped the day before, so it was possible, though it seemed wrong. She tried to remember some rule that forbade sex outdoors or while the sun was up. Nothing came to mind, and she had done such things with her lover. But that had been at festivals and with a woman. Surely sex for procreation ought to be done in a less carefree manner.

He leaned over and kissed the rim of her ear, then touched his tongue to the bare skin inside.

They had sex on the river bluff in a meadow of dry plants. A group of hunting birds soared overhead. At one point, early on, she looked up and saw them, rising in a wide circle. Later, she found she had become preoccupied. The bright open world seemed to darken and turn in upon itself, and she was not aware of much except her body and Eh Shawin's body.

When they had finished, they lay a while together, listening to bugs sing around them.

The birds had gone. Finally, Eh Shawin yawned and sat up. "That's something I haven't done before." He grinned at her. "There's more variety in sex than in war, in my opinion, anyway."

They got up and brushed each other off, then put on their clothing and went to find their *tsina*.

After that, they got in the habit of having sex beyond the town walls. It was the right time of year. The ground was dry, and the biting and burrowing bugs had mostly vanished. Now and then, there was some kind of distraction: a *tsin* would come close while grazing. Once, a fat little *tli* came up to see what they were doing. It stopped just outside reach and reared up on its hind legs, folding its paws against the white fur of its chest.

"Fill your eyes, little trickster," said Eh Shawin.

The animal seemed to listen. It tilted its head and watched them until they were done.

Then, as they moved apart, it moved away.

They still slept in the tower room. By now, she had gotten used to sharing a bed with him. His scent was familiar, and it was comforting to lie against his broad back. Every few days her mother would ask how everything was going.

"Fine," she would answer. Finally she said, "I think I'm like my sister."

Her mother frowned. "In that case, we'll have the man with us all winter. I suppose I shouldn't complain. It gives your cousin someone to practice fighting with."

One morning she woke early and heard the cries of birds as they flew over Ahara Tsal. The fall migrations were beginning. There would be good hunting in the marshes along the river. She prodded Eh Shawin. Half awake, he agreed to go into the valley with her. After breakfast, they saddled their *tsina*.

The morning air was cool, and thin banners of mist floated over the surface of the river. The mist would be gone in less than an *ikun*, and the day would be hot by noon. But at the moment she could feel the sharp edge of autumn. She carried her strung bow. Her quiver hung from her saddle. Eh Shawin had brought a pair of throwing spears. He wasn't really in the mood to kill anything, he told her. "But a ride is fine. I can watch you shoot down birds. And if we encounter anything large, I'll be ready."

There were plenty of animals in the valley, but she didn't see the birds she wanted: the ones she had heard as they flew over. She and Eh Shawin kept going, following a road that wasn't much used. Midway through the morning, two men appeared ahead of them, riding *tsina*. They came out of the underbrush and reined their animals, blocking the road. One had a shield on his arm.

Eh Shawin had been riding in back of her. Now he came up alongside. There was a spear in his hand. "Let me take care of this." She reined Direct Action, and he moved past her. He was riding her young stallion, Hope-for-the-future.

The two men turned their animals so they were facing Shawin, and one drew a sword, a long weapon of war.

Something made a noise in back of her. She glanced around: two more men came riding toward her. They looked like soldiers who had gone to hell: ragged and dirty. One man wore a metal helmet. The other wore a leather cap. They both held battle swords.

She glanced back at Shawin. He'd thrown his spear, and one of the men in front was falling, shouting as he slid onto the ground. The spear was in his chest.

Shawin pulled the second spear from its holder.

The two ragged soldiers came up on either side of her. One glanced over. "We're sorry that this has to happen in front of you, but—as you can see—we're desperate. It will be over quickly." Then they rode on. Direct Action shook his head. She tightened the reins. There was nothing she could do.

Among the *hwarhath*, warfare is entirely a male activity. The *hwarhath* men direct their violence exclusively toward each other. They do no physical harm to women and children, strange as this may sound to humans. But there is a *quid pro quo*. The *hwarhath* teach their women that they must never fight. Eyes-of-crystal knew that she was almost certainly safe. Unless these men were crazy, they would not touch her. But Eh Shawin was going to die, and all the rules of right behavior told her that she had to look on. This was the way it had always been done.

The man of Eh glanced back. He must have seen the two new soldiers. A moment later, he was charging at the man in front of him, spear in hand. Their *tsina* met. Her young stallion screamed, and a man shouted, she didn't know which one. They were tangled together, their animals turning in a circle. The other bandits reined, as if they were trying to see a good way to attack.

There was no way for Eh Shawin to win. His animal was untried. He didn't have the right kind of weapons. A hunting spear and a sword that was little more than a dagger! As ignorant as she was, she knew this was a bad situation. Finally, he was outnumbered. Her male relatives did not speak much about war, but she had heard them say, "As a general rule, big wins over little and many over few."

Eyes-of-crystal pulled an arrow from her quiver. She fit it into her bow and pulled back the string. Hah! This was easy! They were much larger than a bird and hardly moving at all. She let the arrow go. It went into the neck of the man in the leather cap. He screamed, a noise almost like the one made by her young stallion.

The man in the helmet twisted around, a look of horror on his face. "No!" he shouted. Her second arrow went into his chest. Her third went into his throat, and he fell. One foot stayed in its stirrup. He ended on the ground with one leg up. His *tsin* was thin and needed a grooming, but evidently it had been well trained. The moment its rider fell, it stopped moving, except to shake its head. Not that it made any difference. The rider was dead. His *tsin* could have dragged him across the valley and done no further harm.

The man she had shot first, the one in the leather cap, was still on his animal, bent over and holding onto the animal's neck. Blood poured down his back.

Beyond these two, Shawin still struggled with the third man. They were on the ground now, though she hadn't seen how this had happened. Their *tsina* danced around them. The men were entangled. Eyes-of-crystal could not risk a shot.

She waited, bow in hand. The struggle ended, and Eh Shawin stood up. His tunic was torn and dirty. He held his little sword. The blade was covered with blood.

"That seems to be it," Eh Shawin said.

Eyes-of-crystal leaned to one side and vomited.

After she finished, Eh Shawin helped her dismount. He was unharmed, except for a few small cuts. "Though I've been beaten like iron on the anvil, and I'll feel it tomorrow. If your relatives think I am going to be good for much of anything the next few days—"

"I killed them," she said.

"Two of the four."

She went on, speaking disjointedly. How could she tell her relatives? What would they do? No woman of the Ahara had ever gotten involved in a battle.

"None that you have been told about," Eh Shawin said. He turned and watched the one man still alive. His *tsin* had become nervous finally and begun to step sideways like a harvest dancer. Then it shook its body, and the man slid off and lay motionless on the dusty road.

"I'll pull out the arrow and drive in my second spear. It's broken, but no one will know when that happened, and you will have killed only one man then."

That was more than enough, said Eyes-of-crystal.

He tilted his head in agreement, then walked over to the man he had killed with his short sword. "I killed this fellow, then captured his sword." He bent and picked it up. "And used it to kill the last man with two blows, one to the throat and one to the chest. If I make cuts that are big enough, no one will notice the arrow wounds. So two men have died from my spears, one from my short sword and one from this." He lifted the battle sword. "What a hero I am! They'll make up poetry about me in Ahara." He looked at her, meeting her gaze. "And you behaved like a decent woman and watched the fight, never moving a hand."

She spoke again. The story was unlikely. She wasn't a good liar. It would be better to tell the truth.

"If you admit to behavior this unusual, your relatives may decide it wasn't a good idea to breed you," Eh Shawin said in answer. "And if you are pregnant already, they might decide to kill the child. Then all my hard work will have been wasted. I'd prefer that my children live, unless they are damaged in some way.

"And I'd prefer that your life be happy. It isn't likely to be, if you admit to violence. Lie to the best of your ability. That ought to be sufficient. Remember what you have just seen! If you're upset and don't make a lot of sense, your family will understand.

"And while it's unlikely that I could kill four men, my brother has done as much and more. Maybe I had—for once—his determination and power."

She agreed finally, and he did as he had planned, like a manager setting up the opening of a play. Bloodflies had begun to gather, their bodies shining like sparks of fire in the hazy sunlight. He ignored them, cutting the arrow from the one man with his hunting knife. He worked deftly, making the wound only a little larger, then drove in the broken spear, grunting with the effort. Then he moved on to her second victim and used the borrowed battle sword to slash new wounds. The bloodflies hummed around him and crawled on the dead men.

A play would begin with the corpses lying on the stage, looking far more splendid than these fellows. One by one, the corpses would rise, turning into handsome warriors, who would explain to the audience how they came to be in their present situation, acting out the quarrels and moral dilemmas that led to death.

Let nothing like that happen here, said Eyes-of-crystal to the Goddess.

At last Eh Shawin was done preparing the stage. He gathered the men's weapons and loaded them on their *tsina*, then tied the animals to a lead and gave the lead to her. They mounted and rode back toward Ahara Tsal.

They stopped once by a stream. Eh Shawin washed her arrows, which he had kept, then handed them to her.

"I don't want these."

"I don't want them found anywhere close to the place where those fellows died. Someone might wonder. And I can't think of a better place to hide arrows than in a quiver. Get rid of them later."

She put them in her quiver, and they went on.

Hah! It was an event when they arrived at the town, leading four animals, Eh Shawin covered with blood. He did most of the talking, while her relatives comforted her.

Male relatives saddled their *tsina* and rode to find the bodies, led by Shawin. He was fine, he said. A little tired and sore. But he would have no trouble riding back into the valley. The men of Ahara gave him sideways glances that indicated respect.

Her female relatives gave her a bath and put her to bed. After a while, she went to sleep, waking in the middle of the night.

Shawin was settling into bed next to her. She spoke his name.

He said, "We followed their trail back for a distance. There were only the four of them. Bandits, your kinfolk say. Men without a lineage. The world is full of people like that these days. They must have wanted to rob me. The Goddess knows their animals are in bad condition, and they had nothing of value except their battle swords. Hah! To end like that!" Then he went to sleep.

She stayed awake. He had bathed, and he smelled of clean fur and aromatic soap. She found the odor comforting. All at once, she was unwilling to have him leave.

What lay in front of her, after he was gone? Being pregnant and then nursing a child.

Then, maybe, if she could convince her relatives that she had no interest in children, she would be free for a while. That happened sometimes. There were women who could not manage to get interested in

73

motherhood. Other women raised the children they bore.

But if the child turned out well, they would breed her again, maybe to someone like the son of Merin who had fathered her sister's just born child.

And all the while, she would have the secret of her violence in her mind. What if her child was a girl? The trait might be transmitted. She might begin a line of female monsters.

As might be expected, she did not sleep any more that night. In the morning she was queasy and threw up. Not a good sign, the woman thought.

But the next day she was fine, and the day after she and Eh Shawin went riding, though not down into the river valley. Instead they wandered among the fields, now mostly harvested, and went up onto the bluff to their favorite place. They dismounted and sat a while, watching the hunting birds that soared over the valley, circling and chasing one another, not out of anger or from a need to mate, but only (the old women said) for pleasure, from joy in their skill.

Finally Eyes-of-crystal began to speak. She had not been able to shake off her feeling of horror at what she had done, and she did not like to think of living her life with a secret like this one.

"You are not the only person with a secret," Eh Shawin told her gently.

"Not like this," she answered. "And it isn't my secret alone. You know it also."

"I'm not going to tell, dear one."

She glanced at him, surprised. He had used a term that belonged to a lover.

He was lying comfortably full length on the ground, his eyes half closed, his hands folded over his belly. "You are young enough to think that people are the way they appear from the front and that they ought to be so. —What am I? A loyal son of Eh, who carries out an embarrassing obligation as I am told to by the senior women of my lineage?"

"I don't know what to think of you," said Eyes-of-crystal.

"I have never been much interested in sex with men. That is one thing I have in common with my brother, though we differ in our attitude toward sex with women. The idea repels him so much that he has always refused to carry out any breeding contract. I like what I do, though my attitude toward the individual women varies. Still, none of them has ever been stupid, and all of them are in good physical condition."

He smiled at her. "Our lineage has been lucky. They have one son who wants to spend his entire life fighting and killing, which has been very useful, and another son—the twin of Eh Manhata—who is willing to put the same kind of effort into mating.

"And I have been lucky. If my brother had been ordinary, I would spent my life having no sex or sex with men, or I would have become a pervert, sneaking after women. Such men exist, though they are not common, even in this age where everything seems to be unraveling.

"Instead, I am here with you, for which I thank the Goddess and Manhata."

She couldn't think of what to say. They were both monsters, though in different ways.

She had acted in a way that no woman ever should, though she had been unwilling and was now remorseful. His actions were proper. He had done as his female relatives had told him. But his thoughts and feelings were perverse.

"What kind of child is going to come from this mating?" she asked finally.

"I don't know," said Eh Shawin. "But the passing on of traits is not a simple process, as we know from breeding animals as well as people, and we both have many good traits. I think it's likely that the child will be fine."

She looked out at the river valley, then up at the birds, still soaring over the bluffs. A crazy idea came into her mind, and she told it to Eh Shawin.

Why couldn't they go off together? The world was full of people who wandered, having lost their homes in the long war. She could disguise herself like a man. Such things were possible. The actors who came to Ahara Tsal played women convincingly. Or else they could claim to be relatives, a brother and sister. She would not have to hide the person she was from the rest of her family. If the child turned out badly, at least it would not be one of the Ahara. He would not have to go back to the war.

He listened to her patiently. When she finished, he said, "How would we earn a living? I have only two skills, fighting and making women pregnant. The second one would be useless, if I didn't belong to a powerful lineage. As for the first skill, I don't want to become a bandit like those men in the valley."

They could hunt, said Eyes-of-crystal.

"And live like animals in the wilderness?"

They could sell whatever they didn't need, meat and fur.

"Most land is held by some lineage or other. Do you think they'll give us permission to hunt? Do you think people will refrain from asking questions, if we bring the hides of animals into a town? I'd be executed as a thief, and you would be sent off to survive as best you could. Most likely, someone would take you in. Even in this age of unraveling, there are people who will not let a woman come to harm. But you would not be the daughter of a famous lineage, and you would not be loved as you are here.

"And if there were more children, what would happen to them? I don't want my children to be beggars."

"Is there nothing we can do?" asked Eyes-of-crystal.

"What we're doing," said Eh Shawin.

After that she was silent, watching the birds.

It was midwinter before her relatives were certain that she was pregnant. The snow was deep by then, and the winter unusually cold. Eh Shawin stayed on till spring, though she no longer spent time with him. She saw him, now and then, at a distance.

When the thaw was over and roads comparatively dry, he rode off with a group of her male relatives who were returning to the war. She was sick that day and did not see him go. The children were born at harvest time: two boys, large and sturdy. The older became Tsu, which was an old name among the Ahara. The younger became Ehrit, which means "deriving from Eh."

She nursed them for a year, as was customary in those days, then turned them over to one of her sisters and went back to her old habits. But hunting interested her less than it had. She missed having company, and she felt less safe than before. What if other bandits came into the river valley? Would she become violent again? Would they become violent?

Gradually, she became more like other women, though she never became entirely ordinary. She remained more solitary than was usual, and she did not lose her fondness for riding. Now she followed the trails that went through cultivated land, and she kept her eye on the fields and pastures. When she took out a weapon, it was usually to deal with some wild animal that was doing harm to her family's herds and crops.

And though she was not especially maternal, she wasn't able to leave her twins entirely in the hands of her female relatives. Maybe if they had been ordinary, she would have been able to ignore them. But they were clever and active and clearly in front of most other children. When they were two years old, her family bred her again. This time the man came from one of the small lineages that existed at the edges of Ahara.[6] He was solid and handsome with a fine glossy coat, and he did what he was asked to do with determination and competence. But he was obviously embar-

6 The old term for families like this was "side-clingers," though the word can also be translated as "shelf fungus" or even "barnacle." They were too small to survive by their own, so became allies of some large and powerful lineage, which chose not to absorb them for various reasons. Most powerful was the need to have a nearby source for breeding and sexual partners. In the area where this story takes place, the incest taboo forbade—and still forbids—sex of any kind within a lineage. As the lineages grew larger and larger, this began to be a problem, which was solved—at least in part—by the accumulation of clingers.

rassed, and it was clear that he preferred to spend his time with her male relatives. Eyes-of-crystal felt disappointed, though this didn't make any sense. The man behaved exactly as he was supposed to, and he was never discourteous. She got pregnant almost at once. The child was a girl who inherited her father's solidity and lovely fur. What about this mating could cause dissatisfaction?

In time, another gift came from this mating: the man's sister, who was as solid and handsome as her brother and who (unlike him) was comfortable around women. Eyes-of-crystal met her at a festival, and they fell in love. This was (the author tells us) no ordinary casual bed-friendship.

It's important, at this point, to realize that the *hwarhath* tend to see women as less romantic and more promiscuous than men. Living on the perimeter, men have time and opportunity for love. But the women live at the center of the family, surrounded by relatives, and their strongest ties are usually with kin. For women sexual love tends to be a matter of brief couplings at festivals or long-term long-distance romances where the two lovers visit back and forth, but are more often apart than together.

Occasionally, female lovers will move in together, and this has happened much more often in modern times. Conservatives see it as yet another example of how society is going to hell in a hand basket. What is going to become of the People, if women languish and hold onto one another like men? Who is going to look out for the family and the children?

In the age of Eh Manhata this kind of female af-
fection-beyond-the-family was unusual, but it did occasionally happen, and the author of this story, who is
determined apparently to break all the ordinary rules
of romantic fiction, gives her heroine a lover who is
willing to move away from home. The woman was maternal and had no children of her own, the author tells
us, and she found Ahara Pai's children more interesting
than her nephews and nieces.

It's possible that the lover was added to the story
to give it a happy ending. The *hwarhath* insist on happy
endings in their romances, though their idea of a happy
ending is not always the same as ours. Or maybe the
author put the lover in to shock and perturb.

Eyes-of-crystal was bred three more times. Each
time the man was different and came from a different
lineage. The author gives the names of the lineages,
but they would mean nothing to a human reader. Two
were important. One was another clinger. The children—two more girls and a boy—were healthy enough
to keep, and all of them grew to be promising, though
none equaled the twins. They really were exceptional
boys: quick, well-coordinated, intelligent, forceful,
good-humored, and charming.

"This is the spirit of Eh Manhata showing," said
her female relatives.

No, she thought. The intelligence and good humor
came from Eh Shawin. So did the charm, though the
boys were able to get what they wanted from both
women and men. Occasionally she heard news about
Shawin. Her kinfolk took an interest in him now. His
life continued the way he had described it. He was often

away from the army, fulfilling contracts his relatives had made. It seemed as if he almost never failed. The children he fathered were strong and healthy. They made it through the dangerous years of childhood with little trouble. His kinsmen began to call him The Progenitor, and this became the nickname that everyone used.

He was less impressive in the war. Not a bad soldier, her male relatives said, but not what they would have expected from Eh Manhata's twin. "Or from the man who killed those four bandits in our valley. Hah! That was an achievement! We still tell people about it! But he has never done anything comparable."

When the twins were fourteen, there was a festival at Taihanin. Eyes-of-crystal went, along with other women and enough men to provide protection, though the war had moved to the east by now, and all of Ahara and Eh lay between them and the nearest enemy. Her younger children stayed at home, as did her lover, but the twins were old enough for traveling, and they joined the party.

One evening they came to a caravanserai. There were people there already: a small group of soldiers from Eh. One of her male cousins went to speak with the soldiers. When he returned, he said, "Eh Shawin is there. I asked him over. He's never met his sons."

Soon the man himself appeared, walking out of the shadows into the light of Ahara's fire. No question that he had gotten older. He was still tall and rangy, but he moved stiffly now. The fur on his shoulders and upper arms had turned pale silver-grey. But when he saw her, he smiled, and his smile was unchanged: brief but affectionate in a way that was not common among men of the People.

She was right, thought Eyes-of-crystal. The boys got their charm from him.

Her cousin stepped forward and introduced the boys. Eh Shawin looked at them. They had shot up in the last year, and it seemed likely that they would be as tall as he was. At the moment, they were thin and as leggy as *tsina* colts. Like colts, they were nervous and shy. They hung back and ducked their heads, unwilling to meet Eh Shawin's gaze, though they gave him many sideways glances. But there is nothing wrong with shyness in young men and boys, and their manners were good. They answered his questions promptly and clearly, Ehrit doing most of the talking, as he always did.

Finally, Shawin ran out of questions. The boys were given leave to go, and he came over to Eyes-of-crystal. It wasn't required that the two of them talk, but it was permissible.

"You've done a good job," he said.

"My sisters more than I," she said. "And my lover, though I taught the boys to hunt, and that was enjoyable."

He asked if she had other children. She named them and their fathers.

"Your relatives have been keeping you busy," he said.

"Not as busy as the Eh have been keeping you, from what I hear."

He laughed and inclined his head.

They spoke some more about the twins. She praised their qualities, while he looked across the fire. The boys were sprawled on the far side. They had gathered stones and drawn lines in the dirt and were playing a game of strategy. Now and then one or the other would glance up and see Shawin watching, then glance back down.

"So everything has turned out well," Shawin said finally. "You have a lover, and six fine children, and I have my life, which has turned out better than I expected. Hah! I was frightened when I first realized where my sexual interests were likely to lead me.

"I thought, our relatives had been wrong. They worried about Manhata becoming a monster. He was always so relentless, and he cared for so few people, and none of them male. But I was the one who was the monster. I thought, they will find out and kill me, or I will kill myself. But none of that has happened."

"Have you never wanted a lover?" asked Eyes-of-crystal.

He glanced at her sideways and smiled. "How could I have one?—I'll do what I can for your boys when they join the war, though they aren't going to need much help, being Ahara and having the qualities you describe. But I find it pleasant to do what I can."

They said good-by, and he walked back to his campfire, pausing on the way to speak again with his sons.

Eh Shawin lived to be almost eighty, and Eyes-of-crystal reached a hundred, but they never met again, at least so far as the author tells us.

The last part of her story is devoted to the twins, who grew up to be fine soldiers and famous men. When Eh Manhata died at the age of eighty-five, betrayed and murdered by men he trusted, it seemed as if the alliance he had created would be destroyed. It was Ahara Ehrit who held everything together, not through violence, but through negotiation. He was helped (he said) by the fact that the world was full of the children of Eh Shawin. Often, when he met with other lineages, he found that he was talking to a half-brother. And there were certain traits that appeared over and over in Shawin's children. They were reasonable, flexible, good-humored, and willing to make the best of the situation. If they had to, they could fight, but it wasn't their preferred way to solve problems.

Ehrit is known to history as The Negotiator or The Weaver. Eh Manhata began the alliance that finally became the world government, but Ahara Ehrit saved it.

His brother Tsu was better at warfare, and this also was useful to the alliance. He was among the best generals of his generation, though no one in that generation could equal Eh Manhata. Still, Ahara Tsu won most of the battles he fought. His nickname was the Sword of Ahara. In the opinion of Ehrit, his qualities came from their mother. He was more courageous than was typical of the children of Eh Shawin, more relentless, more disciplined, more bloody-minded, and more bent on going his own way, though he always listened to Ehrit, and discipline and loyalty kept him from doing anything seriously off to the side.

Neither of them inherited Eh Manhata's great force of character. But the new age did not need this quality. They both had lovers, men who stayed with them for years, and though both of them fathered children, so far as is known they did so without pleasure.

Two Notes on the Translation

In its upper course the river Tsal is confined by high bluffs of sandstone and limestone, but further to the south and east, it runs between low banks across a level plain. In modern times, engineers have built dams and levees to control it, but in the old days, the river changed course often. Its name comes from these changes in course. Tsal means loose, unfastened, unconnected, wandering, and homeless. Another meaning has been added in the last few years, since the People encountered humanity and the human concept of freedom, which does not (apparently) exist in any *hwarhath* culture. Tsal is the word they use to translate the English word "free." This story, which may be (in part) about freedom, is set by the Loose or Homeless or Untethered or Free River.

In the *hwarhath* main language, there is no way to speak of people without mentioning their gender. The language has singular female, singular male, singular of undetermined gender, female plural, male plural, mixed plural and undetermined plural. There is no mixed plural form of the word lover. Lovers are always both female or both male. The author of this story could have made up a mixed (i.e., heterosexual) form of the word. It would have been recognizable, and her readers would have been shocked. But for once she played it safe, or maybe she wanted her readers to come to the center of the story—its hearth or meaning—slowly. The title she gave the story, assuming that it was given by her and not by a nervous publisher, is best translated into English as "The Breeders." But this title doesn't sound right to humans and distorts the meaning of the story, which is, after all, about love.

Origin Story

Translator's Introduction

Like humanity the *hwarhath* have many origin stories. Most involve a mother goddess. The dominant cultures on the *hwarhath* home planet are monotheistic; and almost all believe their deity is female. After all, they argue, there are animal species that are entirely female and reproduce by parthenogenesis. But no known animal species is entirely male, nor can any male animal produce alone. If the universe reflects its creator, as most creations do, then a male originator of life seems unlikely.

Is it possible to believe in an asexual creator? Yes, and the members of a few small sects do. But most *hwarhath* find the idea as disturbing as the idea of a male creator. A god like a microbe that buds or splits apart? Surely this concept lacks dignity!

In spite of these firmly held and well reasoned ideas about creation, there are anomalous myths. The one that follows is from the *hwarhath* Fifth Continent, the most isolated and peculiar region on the home planet. In it the world does not begin with the considered actions of a wise mother. Instead, it begins with forbidden love and violence. The story's actors are several in number; their actions are ambiguous; and it would be difficult to call any of them—even the Goddess—wise.

In the beginning two things existed. One was a wide, thick sheet of the ice. The other was the sun, which shone on the ice daily. At first it was above the horizon for a brief time only; and the ice did not melt. Then, day by day, it rose higher and remained longer, till it never set. Warmed by continuous sunlight, the ice began to melt. Two forms emerged from it. One was a woman, the other a man. Both had fur the blue-white hue of ice; and their eyes—when these opened—were the color of sunlit sky.

The first thing each saw was the other; and both were immediately filled with lust. When their bodies were completely free of ice, they fell into each other's arms, groping and kissing, like two male or two female lovers. Then they mated, with no bed except ice.

After that they wandered over the ice sheet, looking for something besides themselves. But there was nothing. Ice was their food and drink. They mated often; and the woman began to swell.

All this time, while they wandered and mated and the woman swelled to an ever greater size, the land around them was changing, shaped by thaws and freezes, splitting ice and falling snow. In some places, the land rose into ice-mountains. In other places, it sank into valleys and lakes. When the woman was ready to give birth, she stopped in a valley under a cliff of blue-green ice. Ice rubble lay at the cliff's bottom. Ice boulders were scattered through the valley. On the sides of the boulders opposite the wind, drifts of snow formed. The man shaped one of these into a shelter. He crouched beside the woman, not knowing what else to do. Soon she began to groan with pain.

This was the first birth in the world and among the worst. The woman had no female kin to help her. The man had no idea what was happening. When blood gushed from between her legs, he stood up, crying with horror. As ignorant as he was, he knew the red flood was dangerous. But he did not flee.

Soon a baby followed the blood into sunlight. The man picked her up, marveling at her tiny size and loud voice. She began crying at once.

As he looked at his daughter, a second child—a monster—was born. The moment it arrived in light, it attacked the man. In order to free his hands, and maybe to save his daughter, he tossed the child away. She landed on snow and slid into a deep crevasse. There she lay, lodged between two blue walls, while the monster killed her parents and ate them voraciously. Blood ran into the crevasse. The baby drank it silently.

Opinions vary as to why the second child was a monster. Maybe because the parents had mated improperly. In a sense, they were sister and brother, both born of ice and heat. In addition, their mating had not been arranged—or approved—by senior relatives. They should have asked the ice for permission. If she did not answer, they should have asked the sun. Instead they gave in to an unnatural lust; and lust consumed them during their long journey across the melting ice.

Their purity—for they were surely pure, having been created from ice and sunlight at the beginning of the world—gave them one perfect child. Their lust and lack of consideration made their second child a monster.

This is only one opinion. There are others. Maybe it's the nature of existence to contain both good and bad, beauty and ugliness. Each calls forth the other. Therefore, the perfect child—who became our Goddess—had as her twin a monster.

There are even more opinions, but two are enough for a story as short as this one.

The monster ate every part of its parents, except for the marrow in their bones, the woman's ovaries, and the testicles on the man. It left the bones scattered, not knowing how to break them open or that they contained food. But it buried the ovaries and testicles in snow. Maybe it intended to keep them as a treat later. Then it wandered off and was not seen again for a long time.

The baby grew strong, nourished by her parents' blood. Finally she was able to crawl out of the crevasse. She found her parents' bones scattered across the valley where they'd died. Being magical, she was able to crack the bones and suck out the marrow. This gave her more strength, and she grew to full size.

Imagine her a thick, tall woman, her fur streaked various shades of brown by the blood that had fallen on her in the crevasse. Her eyes are deep orange, the color of the sun when it rises and sets. Her teeth are ice-white.

By taking her parents' blood and flesh into her body, she learned their story. She knew they had been murdered by her twin; and she knew where their sexual organs had been hidden. She dug the organs up. They were hard as stone, a material that did not yet exist. Holding the organs in her hands, the Goddess had an idea. She found some pieces of sinew that her twin had not eaten; these she made into a sling. Then she gathered her parents' split bones. The long ones became spears. The short ones became knives. The pieces that were too small to be knives, she formed into a basket, held together by sinew. She used this to carry her parents' organs, which were too cold to carry in her hands. Finally, she set out to find the monster.

In time she saw it in the distance: a great, hulking, spiny, ugly beast. She came on it from behind, seeing first its twitching tail, then its bony hindquarters, then its forequarters and neck and narrow head. Its long snout was snuffling over the ice, trying to find something—anything—as delicious as its parents.

"Greetings, Twin," the Goddess said, and drove a bone spear into the monster's side. With a roar, it turned and attacked her. They fought for ten days, till the Goddess was streaming blood from many wounds, and numerous spears and knives stuck out of the monster. Finally, as the tenth day ended, the Goddess used her last weapon: the sinew sling. Her father's first testicle hit the monster in the rump, and it staggered. The second testicle hit the monster's side, and her twin stumbled to its knees. Her mother's first ovary hit the monster's shoulder; it fell over. The second ovary hit the monster's skull; it died.

The Goddess gave a yell of triumph. Then she gathered snow to staunch her many wounds. When her bleeding had stopped, she returned to the monster and used its body to build the world we know.

The bony back and backside became mountains. The wide, soft belly became the world's plains and valleys. The monster's hair became vegetation. Its scales became rocks and boulders.

She kept the sun to light her world, but turned most of the ice into water. It became the ocean, rivers, and lakes, though some remains in its original state.

When the world was complete, she put her parents' sexual organs between her thighs and held them there, till they were soft and warm. Then, when they were completely malleable, she used them to form all the world's creatures, including people.

How was she able to imagine a world like this one, when all she had experienced was ice and sunlight and blood? There is no good answer to this question. Maybe the world was somehow implicit in the monster's body and her parents' organs. Maybe the Goddess could see into the future. Her abilities are many and not well understood. If so, she was able to use the world-that-came-into-existence as a model for the world-not-yet-made; and we, living and acting now, may be shaping the world at its moment of origin.

In any case, when she was done, everything was used up, except for the sinew sling. She made it into a bracelet, which she wore on her dominant arm. This is how our oldest statues show her: a broad woman garbed only in her own fur, with no ornament except a narrow bracelet on her left arm or wrist.

The Small Black Box
of Morality

A *Hwarhath* Religious Romance

After the Goddess created the world, she went off to do other things. In time, it occurred to her that she would like to see how the world was doing. So she hiked up her robe and fastened it and crossed the universe with long quick strides, coming at last to the right place.

The world was there, exactly where she had left it. Everything on it flourished, and all the plants and animals behaved as she had intended.

This gave her pleasure, and she decided to spend some time admiring her handiwork. She let down her robe and refastened her belt and stepped out of the sky.

Back and forth she went, over mountains and valleys, across wide prairies and into the ocean. She examined everything and muttered words of praise and self-congratulation. But finally it occurred to her that something was missing.

"None of my plants and animals have any judgment. They can't discriminate. They don't know right from wrong. My world needs morality," the Goddess said.

She took a handful of darkness and shaped it into a box. Into the box she put the ability to tell right from wrong.

Where did she get this ability? Out of herself.

In some versions of the story, this wisdom came from her mouth. It was a small animal that rested on her tongue, and she spat the animal into the box. In other versions, she put blood into the box or milk from her upper left breast. Still other versions claim that she took out her right eye and pulled morality out of her brain through the empty socket. She put the eye back in, but it never saw as sharply after that.

When people behave in a wrong and unjust fashion and get away with it, they are said to live "on the right side of the Goddess."

Wherever it came from, moral judgment was in the box, and the Goddess set out to find someone who wanted her gift.

She went to the trees first. Of all her creatures, they were the least violent and had the most dignity. But they were happy with their slow lives. "Why should we worry about right and wrong? These ideas sound like the chattering animals who live in our branches. They bother us as much as we are willing to be bothered. Leave us, Great Mother, to what you have already given us: sunlight and starlight and rain."

Next she offered her gift to the little plants that covered the ground. But they were happy with their quick lives. "We grow. We flower. We make seeds and die. Surely that is enough, Great Mother. Don't ask us to think as well."

The Goddess turned to her animals. They were all satisfied with what they had already. The predators praised the teeth and claws she had given them. The herd animals praised their horns and quick feet. The sneaky animals were happy with being sneaky. The animals who were good at hiding thanked her for this skill. No one wanted judgment. They all said, "You have provided for us splendidly. We aren't greedy. We don't need anything else."

Finally the Goddess came to the first people. There were only two of them, a woman and a man. The woman was named First Woman. The man was named First Man. At that time, they had no tools and no knowledge of fire. They were not yet hunters. Instead, they wandered through the world looking for things to eat that were small and slow: roots in the ground, bugs and worms. It was a miserable life.

All the fine and handsome animals had turned her down, so the Goddess made her offer to First Woman and First Man.

They listened to her. First Man frowned and looked unhappy. As bad as his life was, he was used to it. Morality was an innovation. That bothered him.

But First Woman said, "It's worth a try. As animals go, we aren't much to speak of. We are small and slow and lack the abilities that other animals have. We aren't even attractive. Look at the fur that covers us! It's a very ordinary shade of gray, and it isn't especially thick or soft or glossy. Many animals have coats that are much handsomer.

"The same is true of every part of us. Our teeth can't tear like the teeth of a predator, and they can't grind like the teeth of an animal that grazes. Our nails are blunt. We can't see half as well as that hunting bird in the sky."

"Where? Where?" asked First Man and peered upward.

First Woman ignored him. "Our hearing is not especially keen. Our sense of smell is worse than our sense of hearing.

"If we take this gift, which the Great Mother has offered us, at least we'll be different. And maybe the Goddess will take an interest in us. Maybe she will help us now and then."

First Man scratched his crotch and picked his nose and tried to think of an argument. But nothing came to him, since he lacked judgment and discrimination.

So the woman held out her hand, and the Great Mother put the small black box of morality on her palm.

The woman opened the box, though it wasn't easy, since she lacked judgment and had never seen a box before. Inside was the ability to think about ideas. She took it out and divided it. Since she was bigger than the man, she took the piece that was larger and ate it greedily.

First Man turned his piece over and over and sniffed it and touched it with the tip of his tongue.

By this time, the woman had judgment, and she knew that it hadn't been a good idea to take the bigger piece, since it meant that First Man would always have a less good sense of morality. But what's done is done.

"Eat it up," she said and praised the wonderful flavor of the thing and how full she was now and how satisfied she felt. This was not all entirely true, but she knew that people had no future, unless both sexes could tell right from wrong.

Finally, the man ate his piece of morality.

"What happens after this ought to be interesting," said the Goddess.

Writing Science Fiction
during the Third World War

Guest of Honor Speech, WisCon, May 2004

What follows is a description of what I've been reading and thinking during the past couple of months, while watching the war in Iraq play out over the Internet.

I'm going to start with some ideas from Immanual Wallerstein, a sociologist who has clearly been influenced by Marxism, though I don't know if he would call himself a Marxist.[1]

According to Wallerstein, we are living within a political and economic system which originated in Europe about 500 years ago, but is now worldwide. Politically this system is characterized by nation states. Its economic form is capitalism.

1   My understanding of Immanuel Wallerstein comes from
    The Decline of American Power: The US in a Chaotic World
    (New York, The New Press, 2003).

Wallerstein believes this world system is now in crisis, a crisis from which it will not recover. I'm not sure I entirely agree with his reasons for the economic crisis, though I do agree that capitalism is in trouble.

What I find interesting is Wallerstein's analysis of what's happening to nation states.

First, he argues that capitalism—for all that capitalist thinkers thunder against government interference—*needs* national governments. Nation states provide capitalists with protection in the form of patents, copyrights, tariffs, and armies. They create an infrastructure which capitalists may not want to build themselves but are happy to use. Examples in the US are the railroads, funded by huge government land grants; the interstate highway system, built during the Cold War with tax money; and the Mississippi River, which the Army Corps of Engineers has turned into a barge canal. I have spent my life on the Mississippi. A lot of freight gets moved along it—and through the St. Lawrence Seaway, another government project.

Nation states fund R&D, turning the results over to manufacturers under cost or for free. They funnel large amounts of money into specific industries, such as war industries. And they control what were called in the 19th century "the dangerous classes"—poor and working people. Part of this control is direct, through cops and prisons. But the so-called advanced or western nations also provide services—education, health care, pensions—which make life more tolerable and citizens less desperate.

Finally, nation states provide hope, which Wallerstein argues may be their most effective form of control. For more than two hundred years, since the English and American and French revolutions, people have seen the possibility of using national governments to improve their lives, sometimes through revolution, more often through the expansion of suffrage, the creation of political coalitions, and the making of laws.

This era—when people hoped to make a better future by gaining control of the state through election or revolution—ended in the late 20th century, according to Wallerstein. By this time, Russia and China had demonstrated that revolutionary states did not provide people with peace, justice, and freedom. The Social Democratic states of western Europe demonstrated that elected socialists were unable to deliver on the promises of socialism. And the postcolonial states of Asia, Africa, and Latin America failed to achieve humane postcolonial societies. Nations of every kind remained enmeshed in a world system dominated by capitalism's drive to accumulate wealth, no matter what the cost to humanity and the planet. My own private image of capitalism and capitalists is the great white shark—a primitive animal, in many ways limited, but very good at what it does. One cannot build a humane society on a base of great white sharks.

According to Wallerstein, because the world system of nation states has failed to deliver a decent life for most people, it has lost credibility. People no longer see the state as a tool to be used to improve human existence.

For him, the key year is 1968, when there were revolutions in France and Czechoslovakia, a brutally suppressed student uprising in Mexico, and violent struggles against war and racism in the US. The late 60s is when the American cities burned. If you're too young to remember or weren't living in a burning city, I recommend *Dhalgren* by Samuel R. Delany, a terrific portrait of big American cities in the late 60s. Detroit in 1968 and 69 was exactly like *Dhalgren*. Even the poets were the same.

France, Czechoslovakia, Mexico, and America are the struggles I know about. Wallerstein says there were others worldwide. According to him, these were not efforts to seize the state, but struggles against the state, against all states and the very idea of states.

He's arguing that ideas have power. As long as people believe in the state as something worth having, they will work to maintain a state apparatus. At the very least, they will obey laws. When they give the state up as hopeless and useless, its ability to survive is threatened.

One example of this is the collapse of the Soviet Union and the eastern block. The second most powerful nation on Earth simply fell apart, with remarkably little violence for a change so huge.

Another example may be the US, where the current administration appears to dismantling the federal government. This isn't being done accidentally. Grover Norquist, a conservative thinker and mentor for the Bush Administration, has said that he wants to weaken the federal government until it can be dragged into the bathroom and drowned in the bathtub. Pat Robertson has advocated nuking the US State Department. These people aren't kidding. Their language may be colorful, but they mean what they say.

Why are they bent on destroying the federal government, if capitalism needs nation states? Short term, they will be rid of many tiresome government regulations, and the opportunities for stealing of publicly owned resources will be huge. Long term—I suspect Pat Robertson is already working on plans for a new Christian government to succeed the US of A.

If Wallerstein is right, the next 50 years of human history will be a period of breakdown and chaos. It won't be a comfortable period. It's likely to be dangerous. It's also likely to be full of possibility. A stable system is almost impossible to change, according to Wallerstein. Huge efforts produce very small results. The system always tends to restabilize. But when a system is breaking down and off-balance, a small effort can create large changes. I think Wallerstein is influenced by chaos theory here, and the gentle flapping you hear in the background is the famous Amazonian butterfly.

The end of the crisis is not certain. The new society which emerges may be as bad or worse than the one we live in now. The kind of theocracy described in *Native Tongue* and *The Handmaid's Tale* seems much more possible to me than it did a few years ago. But if we think and act—we in general, the human race—we may be able to create a new society that is genuinely decent. According to Wallerstein, *now* is the time to think about what kind of society we want to emerge from chaos— and what we are going to do to create that new society.

✦

I am going to move now to the ideas of William S. Lind, Director of the Center for Cultural Conservatism at the Free Congress Foundation. Lind is, as his title suggests, a conservative. I suspect he and I don't have a lot in common. But he has some interesting things to say about modern warfare.

He divides modern war into four generations, beginning in the mid-seventeenth century in Europe. I'm going to skip the first three generations, except to say that in all three wars were fought by conventional armies, employed by and controlled by nation states.

Fourth Generation warfare is radically different. In some ways, it is guerrilla warfare, but unlike the American Revolution—an early example of a modern guerrilla war—Fourth Generation warfare is not controlled by a state. It is decentralized, carried on by what might be called non-governmental organizations. At times, as in Iraq now, the organization is so loose that one isn't sure an organization exists.

At this point, I'm going to quote Lind.

> All over the world, state militaries find themselves fighting non-state opponents... Almost everywhere, the state is losing...

> At [the] core of [Fourth Generation warfare] lies a universal crisis of the legitimacy of the state, and that crisis means many countries will evolve Fourth Generation war on their soil. America, with a closed political system... and a poisonous ideology of 'multiculturalism' is a prime candidate for the homegrown variety of Fourth Generation war.[2]

I don't agree with Lind that multiculturalism is poisonous. But I agree with him that the collapse of the official, white, Christian, flag-waving, Indian-kill-

2   William S. Lind, "Understanding Fourth Generation War," January 15, 2005, Antiwar.com.

ing, Fourth-of-July American culture is dangerous to the status quo. That culture is what makes all of us—oppressors and the oppressed—a single, unified nation. It legitimates our government and our economic system.

Now for another quote. It's from an essay by Prince El Hassan bin Talal of Jordan, which appeared in the *Toronto Globe and Mail* on April 7, 2004.

> There are more than forty so-called low-intensity conflicts in the world today. Maybe it is not the Third World War if you are living in Manchester or Stockholm, but if I were living in Madrid when in the bombs at the station went off, it would seem very much like the Third World War to me.

As soon as I read this, I thought, "Yes. The prince is right. We *are* living in the middle of the Third World War."

✦

To sum up, if these three very different men are correct, the near future is likely to be a period of collapsing governmental structures and warfare so widely spread that it can be called a World War. Much that is bad may result from this era of collapse and violence: the rise to power of right-wing religious movements, the reversion to a world comprised of tribes and tribal loyalties. The position of women may well worsen. We've already seen ethnic cleansing in the former Yugoslavia, genocide in Rwanda, and something between ethnic cleansing and genocide in Palestine.

✦

Is there a bright side to this dark vision of the future? Do I see hope anywhere? Yes.

Political and social struggles worldwide—struggles I would call progressive—are increasingly aware of one another and connected, via the mass media and the Internet. I have been following the war in Iraq through Internet postings by independent reporters and peace activists now in the country, as well as posting by Iraqis, especially the wonderful Riverbend, an Iraqi woman currently living in occupied Baghdad. I strongly recommend her weblog *Baghdad Burning* (http://riverbendblog.blogspot.com/).

I'm going to talk briefly about a few of these struggles, starting with the Zapatista Liberation Army. This is an organization of poor Native American farmers, living in the mountains of Chiapas in southern Mexico. It emerged into public view on January 1, 1994—the same day that the North American Free Trade Agreement took effect. From the start, the Zapatistas have addressed themselves to the world. Their remarkable PR man, Subcommandante Marcos, appears to have spent the past ten years in the Mexican jungle, armed with a computer, modem, and satellite dish. His manifestoes are wonderfully eloquent, clever, and funny. There's a rumor that Marcos has an advanced degree in mass communications. The university that trained him ought to advertise. "You too can charm and amaze the world."

I'm going to quote from the "First Declaration of *La Realidad* for Humanity and Against Neoliberalism," issued two years after the Zapatistas first appeared the world stage.

A new lie is being sold to us as history. The
lie of the defeat of hope, the lie of the defeat
of dignity, the lie of the defeat of humanity...
In place of humanity, they offer us the stock
market index. In place of dignity, they offer us
the globalization of misery. In place of hope,
they offer us emptiness. In place of life, they
offer us an International of Terror. Against
the International of Terror...we must raise an
International of Hope. Unity, beyond borders,
languages, colors, cultures, sexes, strategies,
and thoughts, of all those who prefer a living
humanity. The International of Hope. Not the
bureaucracy of hope, not an image inverse to,
and thus similar to, what is annihilating us.
Not power with a new sign or new clothes. A
flower, yes, (the) flower of hope.[3]

Starting in 1999, a series of internationally organized demonstrations protesting globalization have
occurred at almost every meeting of the World Trade
Organization.

Globalization is a slippery and dishonest word. It has
nothing to do with internationalism; it is an attempt to
remove national and local barriers to the movement of
capital, and national and local limitations to the power
of capital. This includes laws protecting the environ-
ment, natural resources, and workers. If the WTO has
its way, nothing will be safe from the sharks.

The first in the series of demonstrations—the Battle in Seattle in 1999—shut down the WTO's Third
Ministerial Meeting. The ministers simply could not
go on. Since then, WTO meetings in Prague, Genoa,

3 First Declaration of *La Realidad* for Humanism and Against
Neoliberalism," www.ezln.org.

Montreal, and Cancun have been met with demonstrations made up of labor union members, farmers, environmentalists, students, and indigenous people from all over the world. The most powerful people on Earth meet to divide the Earth up, and they can't do it unless they hunker down behind a wall of cops, concrete, and razor wire. There is no place on Earth where the rich and powerful are truly safe.

The most recent meeting in Cancun ended in failure, due to a rebellion of Southern Hemisphere nations, led by President Luiz Ignacio Lula da Silva of Brazil. As far as I can tell from news reports, the demonstrations—and especially the protest-suicide of one of the demonstrators, a South Korean farmer—helped the southern hemisphere representatives hold firm.

The future of the WTO is currently uncertain.

We now come to the Invasion of Iraq and the world-wide peace demonstration held just before the Invasion. This was an amazing event. Something like ten million people marched in Europe, Asia, Africa, and the Americas. The US coverage was not good, so I read Internet editions of English, French, Cuban, and Mexican papers. There were demonstrations in Malaysia, Bangladesh, India, the Middle East, most Latin American countries, I no longer remember which countries in Africa—all acting in concert, all aware of one another.

I will end this catalog of resistance with a simple observation. Whenever people demonstrate anywhere about anything, some of their signs are in English. People no longer speak only to their locality or nation. They address the entire world.

Do I have any idea where this new international consciousness will lead? Or whether the current international struggles for peace and against capital will produce a better world? No, of course not. I am simply indicating that—as the chief defenses of the old society, nation states and national armies, lose power—a loose, worldwide organization is taking form. It has a decentralized structure and is run from the bottom up. It may represent a new kind of social structure, or it may be a dead end. I have no idea how it will develop or if it will develop at all.

The world is still full of nuclear weapons. AIDS is killing much of Africa and spreading through the former Soviet Union, along with multi-drug-resistant TB. We are running out of fresh water. Our soil is degrading. Hundreds of millions of people live in dire poverty, at the edge of starvation. Right now, the starvation is due to poverty, not absolute lack of food worldwide. But Earth's farmers have not produced enough food to feed humanity for the past four years. We've been making up the difference with stockpiled food. This cannot continue indefinitely—or for long.

Petroleum production may be peaking right now, at a time when the demand for oil and gas is rising worldwide. Royal Dutch Shell just wrote down their petroleum reserves. They had been lying about how much oil they had. Who else may be lying? I read one expert who has doubts about the Saudi oil reserves.[4]

I haven't even gotten to the Greenhouse Effect.

4 "Get Ready for $50 US Oil!!" *Energy Bulletin*, June 15, 2004 and "Shell Cuts Oil and Gas Reserves for the Fifth Time," *Energy Bulletin*, February 5, 2005.

We are living in an age of revolution *and* in a science fiction disaster novel. No, we are living in several science fiction disaster novels at once. The stakes are huge. Human civilization may be at risk. The solutions are going to require science and technology, as well as political and social struggle.

What are we—as science fiction readers and writers—doing about this? Historically, science fiction has been about big problems, use and misuse of technology, the broad sweep of history, and every kind of change. Historically, it has been a cautionary and visionary art form. Are we continuing this tradition? Are we writing books that accurately reflect our current amazing and horrifying age? Are we talking about the kind of future we want to see and how to begin creating it?

Or are we, in the immortal words of the preacher in *Blazing Saddles*, just jerking off?

✦ ✦ ✦

I gave the above speech in May of 2004. What can I add eleven months later?

The problems listed have not gone away. To give three examples from March 2005…

On March 30, the Millennium Ecosystem Synthesis Report was released. According to the report, 60% of the world's ecosystems are being degraded or used unsustainably, leading to the increasing likelihood of abrupt changes that affect human well-being. Among these changes are new diseases, sudden changes in water quality, creation of dead zones along coasts, collapse of fisheries, and shifts in regional climate.

"Abrupt" and "sudden" are scary, science-fictional words.

On March 31, the International Energy Agency released a new emergency plan, to be put into effect if world oil production drops 1-2%, as it did during the oil lockout in Venezuela in 2002 and the Iraq invasion of 2003. The plan includes reduced speed limits, driving bans, free public transportation, and a shorter work week. The plan is only a suggestion. Nations need not comply. But the plan suggests that the IEA no longer believes that the world's oil industry can compensate for disruptions.

As with the ecological changes, we are looking at sudden crisis, rather than slow and graceful change: more evidence that we now live in a science fiction disaster novel.

On March 23, 2005, the Indian parliament amended Indian patent law to conform with the World Trade Organization's TRIPS (trade-related aspects of intellectual property rights) regime.

This doesn't sound especially dramatic. Why does it matter?

The generic anti-viral drugs that are used to treat AIDS in poor countries come mostly from India, where national law has permitted pharmaceutical companies to analyze and copy patented drugs. The Indian manufacturers sell their anti-viral drugs at a fraction of the price charged by the American and European patent-holders. According to the *New York Times*, Indian exports to Africa helped drive the cost of AIDS drugs down from $15,000 a year to $200 a year.[5]

5 "India Alters Law on Drug Patents," *New York Times*, March 24, 2005.

As of March 23, Indian manufacturers must pay royalties to patent-holders, which will increase the price of their drugs; and the law makes copying new drugs more difficult and expensive. It's almost certain that people will die because of this change in Indian patent law.

Obviously corporations are going to protect their patents, even though people die. No one in his or her right mind would argue that capitalism is inherently moral. The argument since the 18th century has been: private individuals working for their own personal benefit, untouched by altruism and uninterested in the happiness of others, will create a greater good for all.

In a world where natural resources, including water, are diminishing, international business makes the obvious decision: get control of the resources. If water is running short, you can make money selling it. If oil is running out, sell as much as you can as fast as you can.

This brings us to the struggle against business as usual.

In Bolivia in 2003, massive demonstrations, work stoppages, and transportation blockages forced President Gonzalo Sanchez de Lozado to resign and flee to the United States. The key issues were privatization of water, oil, and gas and the proposed construction of a pipeline. The pipeline would take Bolivian natural gas to Chile, where it would be shipped to California. The Bolivian people would lose a valuable natural resource, which could be used to develop their desperately poor country; and—thanks to privatization—their government would not get a fair price for the gas.[6]

6　The government's share of oil and gas revenues dropped from 50% to 18% after privatization.

Bolivians had seen this before. Starting in the sixteenth century, a huge fortune in silver and tin was taken out of Bolivia, leaving the native population with nothing.[7] The Bolivians did not want to lose another fortune. They took to the streets. They are still in the streets in April 2005, demonstrating against the current president Carlos Mesa.

In Venezuela, Hugo Chavez—a democratically elected, populist president—has been engaged in a multiyear struggle to keep his job. A coup d'etat in April 2002 failed when hundreds of thousands of Venezuelans demonstrated in support of Chavez; he was returned to power after 48 hours.

In December 2002 the management of the Venezuelan state oil company staged a lockout and shutdown, demanding that Chavez resign. This "general strike" against Chavez did not spread beyond the largely white upper and middle classes and ended in failure. Chavez fired the oil company managers.

The opposition then began collecting signatures for a referendum on Chavez. In 2004 he won the referendum and was confirmed in office. His position is not entirely secure, given the hostility of the US government. But for the time being, he is proceeding as he

7   The silver mine at Potosi in Bolivia produced 137 million pounds of silver between 1545 and 1835. This amazing wealth funded much of the economic development of Europe. The silver was mined by Indian and African slaves. It's estimated that the average miner lasted six months before he died, and that eight million workers died in Potosi. Though largely depleted, the mine is still worked today. Contemporary miners usually begin working in their teens, though there are younger workers in the mine. Their life expectancy is 40.

promised: to use the oil wealth of Venezuela for the benefit of ordinary Venezuelans, who are desperately poor people of Native American and African descent.

In late 2004, the citizens of Uruguay elected their first left-of-center president ever and passed a constitutional reform defining water as a public good and guaranteeing public participation at every level of water management.

Comparable struggles against water privatization are occurring in India, where Coke is depleting water tables in farming districts to make bottled water for the Indian domestic market.

Two things should be noted about these struggles. (1) They are largely nonviolent. (2) Instead of a vanguard party or guerilla army, they involve mass demonstrations, work stoppages, barricades on roads, and elections. In addition, there are recurring issues: the right to honest elections, popular control of natural resources, and the right of ordinary people to stay alive.

What does this have to do with Immanuel Wallerstein's theory that the state lost credibility after 1968?

President Sanchez de Lozado fled Bolivia because of mass demonstrations against the state. President Hugo Chavez retained his position in Venezuela due to popular interventions in the business of the state and the political classes. We can add the demonstrations against the WTO; worldwide peace marches in 2003; mass demonstrations in Spain after the Madrid train bombing and the government's attempt to lie about the bombing; mass demonstrations in Georgia, the Ukraine, and Kyrgyzstan after possibly corrupt elections; and mass demonstrations in Iraq against the occupation. Apparently there are many people in the world who are unwilling to let the state make decisions for them. As the wonderful movie *Chicken Run* says, "The chickens are revolting."

Chicken Run came out in 2000 and must have been in production prior to 1999, so we can't call it a post-Seattle movie. Maybe it's a Zapatista movie. Instead of taking over the farm, as Orwell's animals did, the chickens escape and establish a new democratic society, similar (it can be argued) to the self-governing "autonomous villages" that came into existence in Chiapas in the 1990s. The Zapatistas say explicitly that they don't want to seize power. Instead, they want to exercise power where they are in the villages of Chiapas.

Is this a revolution? Not yet. Will it become one? I don't know. But I do not think corporations—and the governments which represent them—will give up business as usual; and I find it hard to believe that billions of people will go quietly into death so business as usual can continue.

✦

I'm going to end this with a quote from China Mieville, from the *Nebula Awards Showcase 2005*. He is talking about his particular sub-genre of sf, called New Weird. I know nothing about New Weird, but I like his vision of what science fiction can be:

> It's my opinion that the surge in the un-escapist, engaged fantastic, with its sense of limitless potentiality and the delighted bursting of boundaries, is an expression of a similar opening up of potentiality in "real life," in politics. Neoliberalism collapsed the social

imagination, stunting the horizons of the possible. With the crisis of the Washington Consensus and the rude grassroots democracies of the movements for social justice, millions of people are remembering what it is to imagine. That's why New Weird is post-Seattle fiction.[8]

8 *Nebula Awards Showcase 2005* (New York, Roc, 2005) p. 50.

Books by Eleanor Arnason

The Sword Smith
Condor Press, 1978
Ebook release, Aqueduct Press, 2015

To the Resurrection Station
Avon Books, 1986
Ebook release, Aqueduct Press, 2015

Daughter of the Bear King
Avon Books, 1987
Ebook release, Aqueduct Press, 2015

A Woman of the Iron People
William Morrow, 1993

Ring of Swords
Tor Books, 1993

Tomb of the Fathers
Aqueduct Press, 2010

Mammoths of the Great Plains
PM Press, 2010

Big Mama Stories
Aqueduct Press, 2013

Hidden Folk: Icelandic Fantasies
PM Press, 2014

Hwarhath Stories: Transgressive Tales by Aliens
Aqueduct Press, 2016

About the Author

Eleanor Arnason was born in Manhattan and grew up in New York, Chicago, London, Paris, Washington DC, Honolulu, St. Paul, and Minneapolis. She received a BA in art history from Swarthmore College and did graduate work at the University of Minnesota, before quitting to learn about life outside art museums and institutions of higher learning. She made her first professional sale in 1972 while living in the Detroit inner city. Since then she has published five novels and over thirty works of short fiction. Her fourth novel, *A Woman of the Iron People*, won the James Tiptree Jr. award for gender-bending science fiction and the Mythopoeic Society Award for adult fantasy. Her fifth novel, *Ring of Swords*, won a Minnesota Book Award. Since 1994 she has devoted herself to short fiction. Her story "Dapple" won the Spectrum Award for GLBT science fiction and was a finalist for the Sturgeon Award. Other stories have been finalists for the World Fantasy, Hugo, and Nebula Awards.

She lives in Minnesota, where she makes her living as the financial manager for a small arts nonprofit. Aside from accounting and science fiction, her interests include politics, economics, bird watching, driving down two-lane country highways, and exploring the remains of the Great Lakes industrial belt.

In spite of all setbacks and adversity, she remains a lifelong fan of ordinary human decency and the international working class.

Made in the USA
Monee, IL
13 September 2022

13858312R00080